everyday raw desserts

everyday **raw desserts**

matthew kenney

photographs by adrian mueller

GIBBS SMITH
TO ENRICH AND INSPIRE HUMANKIND

First Edition
14 13 12 11 10   5 4 3 2 1

Text © 2010 Matthew Kenney
Photographs © 2010 Adrian Mueller

Published by
Gibbs Smith
P.O. Box 667
Layton, Utah 84041

1.800.835.4993 orders
www.gibbs-smith.com

Gibbs Smith books are printed on paper produced from
sustainable PEFC-certified forest/controlled wood source.
Learn more at: www.pefc.org
Printed and bound in Hong Kong

Library of Congress Cataloging-in-Publication Data

Kenney, Matthew.
 Everyday raw desserts / Matthew Kenney ;
photographs by Adrian Mueller. — 1st ed.
     p. cm.
 Includes index.
 ISBN-13: 978-1-4236-0599-7
 ISBN-10: 1-4236-0599-3
 1. Desserts. 2. Raw foods. I. Title.
 TX773.K45 2010
 641.8'6—dc22

                    2010001325

CONTENTS

acknowledgments

In the romantic sense, the term "chef" implies an individual, mastering a kitchen and whipping up magical recipes to an adoring public. In reality, the art of cooking on a professional level is also about team building and developing working relationships with like-minded, talented individuals who will add to, or even enhance, the end result of your efforts.

Since my very first days working with food, I have had the good fortune to collaborate with many unique people, all of whom have contributed to, supplemented, or guided my direction. That is especially true of cookbooks I have authored.

During the entirety of the development of *Everyday Raw Desserts*, Meredith Baird has been carrying out the vision for this book, carefully crafting, testing, researching, and otherwise bringing to life the many unique recipes and processes that it includes.

My gratitude goes out to her, not only for this commitment, but also for the gift of the talent she offered to the process. Without Meredith, you would not be so close to enjoying a number of amazing raw desserts. Her imprint is on every recipe and page of this book.

I also thank Adrian Mueller, a wonderful photographer and human being, for his patience, dedication, and ability to work through a week of driving rain on the Maine coast—our next shoot will have sun!

Jessica Acs, who flew to Maine from Canada to join our photo shoot, provided the perfect balance of peace and added energy needed to produce 50 raw dishes in just a few days. Your cupcakes rocked!

The production of a cookbook is a finely tuned process, much like theatre. Many components provide challenges and the navigation, coordination, and decision making of putting a book together all require extraordinary talent. Many thanks to my talented editor, Jennifer Adams, who has guided two of my previous books, *Everyday Raw* and *Entertaining in the Raw*, and now *Everyday Raw Desserts*.

Also, to Gibbs Smith and the entire team at Gibbs Smith for their ongoing commitment to creating beautiful and meaningful books.

Finally, I would like to thank all of my business partners, Roman Schatzby, Dara Prentice, Raymond Azzi, and many others who believe in, and support, the ongoing commitment we all share toward enhancing the world of sustainable cuisine.

introduction

Everyone familiar with the raw food world knows the poorly kept secret of how rich, decadent, and colorful its desserts can be. In fact, aside from its many well-documented health benefits, desserts may be raw food's biggest asset. In my own transition to a vegan lifestyle, it certainly made the path much more appealing once I learned that I would still be surrounded by more pies, tarts, cookies, cakes, and chocolate than one could ever imagine. The presence of desserts has been prominent since my initiation, although it has only been recently that I have grown to understand the incredible potential of these sweet creations.

When I first started working with living cuisine, before even owning a Vita-Mix or having opened a young coconut, raw desserts were pretty straightforward, slightly heavy and often including some non-raw ingredients. Agave nectar wasn't as popular as it is today, and raw cacao powder was just becoming readily available, so we still used cocoa powder or carob for chocolate recipes, and refined, original techniques to use as reference were few and far between. A few years of working with the plant-based cuisine, and affiliations with several talented chefs have elevated the results of the cuisine I am involved with. No aspect better represents this creative growth than desserts.

It wasn't until I discovered raw food that I found I could thoroughly appreciate desserts, at least in the way that I do now. Refined sugar, flour, and dairy products render desserts not only bland (to a palate accustomed to pure, clean flavor) but also unhealthy and certainly not providing the guiltless pleasure found in raw desserts. Just as I did in my prequel to this book, *Everyday Raw,* I am fully understanding of the challenges we face to prepare delicious raw food at home, with a limited amount of kitchen time available. The recipes in this book recognize the need for streamlining and are designed for efficiency. Although many still involve several steps, which elevated raw food always does, they are organized in such a way that most can be quickly assembled and easily stored.

These new recipes also take into account the way we like to eat at home on a regular day, usually in a casual manner, without a lot of fuss and service requirements. The majority of these dishes can be made well ahead of time, and, once prepared, can be served in a matter of seconds. The one bit of advice I always offer is that, as a home cook, you should always view a recipe as a guide, rely on it as much as necessary, but also feel free to use your own intuition if you prefer something a little more or less sweet, richer, softer, or otherwise different than what the book recommends. Ingredients are not always identical, climates change our tastes, and every palate is different than the other, so try to be flexible and enjoy the process, especially when you get to eat.

MY DESSERT PHILOSOPHY

There are many characteristics that inspire me when considering what I love about raw desserts, but one stands out more than the others: seasonality. Seasons are my guiding force for all cuisine, whether it is desserts or savory dishes. I believe in food that looks as good as it tastes, and vice versa. Presentation is not everything but it counts for a lot, especially when preparing meals for others. Although I do enjoy an abstract dessert on a special occasion, I tend to like comfortable recipes, with a modest number of ingredients and components. Ultimately, the same words that have influenced my work for years, *clean* and *sexy,* along with *light,* when possible, continue to guide what I really like.

High quality, seasonal, organic ingredients at their freshest are the building block of any great cuisine. We spend nearly as much energy searching for great products as we do preparing them. Although a dish that may have been prepared with a few minor errors can still taste great if the ingredients are all superior, no amount of culinary skill can ever mask inferior, under-ripe, or poor quality products. For that reason, I believe in building a network of suppliers to source your favorite ingredients. We are fortunate to live in areas where we have access to all the best ingredients. Although we do use a number of regional or seasonal products here, we have tried to provide options for them that will allow you to make substitutions as needed. Other ingredients may not be locally available, but everything in this book is easily accessible online if not locally.

More than ever before, I believe in respecting geographical recipes and classic flavor combinations. Nothing about raw food is classic, but we do make an effort to present food that, although in an entirely new form, still tastes familiar and is pleasant, never shocking. Raw food is new to many, and in the end, it is part of a meal to be enjoyed, rather than experimented with. There is nothing better than seasonal fruits, so we have worked to keep summer and fall recipes including them as simple as possible, allowing the fruit to be served in its natural state; heavier winter dishes often include more elaborate and bold flavor components.

HOW TO USE THIS BOOK

My goal for *Everyday Raw Desserts* is to show how refined, restaurant-quality desserts can be prepared easily and in as little time as possible. As with all of my books, I suggest reading it from cover to cover—it will only take a couple of hours!—and giving thought to the frequently used techniques in each chapter, as well as the foods that inspire you. Then, prepare something that seems comfortable and simple, a dish you can't wait to eat and serve to friends and family. As you get more comfortable with the elements of the book, try experimenting by substituting ingredients, adapting and adjusting as desired. In the end, it will hopefully add to your enjoyment of raw food and of preparing it for others.

EVERYDAY RAW DESSERT HANDBOOK

In just a few years, millions of people, including myself, have gone from never hearing about raw food, to fully understanding it, in concept at least. Whereas when I began preparing it, I was constantly asked what it consisted of, I now meet large groups of people, all of whom are familiar with it. I recently hosted a raw food event in my hometown in Maine, perhaps one of the last places one would expect raw food to become popular. When I asked the group of seventy who was unfamiliar with the cuisine, not a single hand was raised. This has happened to me several times in the past couple of years, which leads me to believe that most people who are or will become interested in raw food have access to plenty of information about its many attributes, both on a health and culinary level.

For this reason, I continue to direct my energies on my passion to pursue culinary progress, to find and create foods that are unique, flavorful, and that will add to the overall culinary landscape of options available to the public. When it comes to raw desserts, my mission as an author is very straightforward: to provide others with the skills, techniques, and food pairing guidelines that will give them the comfort and ability they need to produce the highest level of cuisine at home.

Fortunately, the same equipment used for savory raw food is what we employ when preparing raw desserts. Ingredients are, for the most part, even easier to understand and far fewer in number. Techniques vary a bit, but we have worked hard to define them in an understandable way. With a firm grasp on these aspects of the cuisine, you will be comfortable and on your way to many great dishes.

TOOLS OF THE TRADE

Raw desserts are prepared with many of the same components of other desserts—the usual suspects such as a sharp knife, paring knife, cutting board, rolling pin, mixing bowls, blender (preferably a Vita-Mix), and food processor are the most frequently used. In any kitchen where you hope to prepare desserts on a regular basis, there is always a need for a variety of tart and pie molds, cake pans, chocolate molds, muffin tins, and loaf pans.

We make an effort to standardize our recipes to make it easier for you at home—most of our cakes are baked in 9-inch pans, as opposed to a variety of sizes, shapes, or even individual options. Of course, you can easily adapt recipes to suit other sizes, but if you are like us, kitchen space is valuable and equipment is sometimes scarce.

Aside from the basics, it is definitely worthwhile to source tart, cake, and other pans that have removable bottoms. Raw foods are often more delicate due to the lack of flour and other binding ingredients and therefore benefit from this convenience. These pans are highly recommended for a more sophisticated presentation. Most recipes, however, can be adapted or adjusted to fit nearly any tart or cake pan.

KEY PRODUCTS

The good news about shopping for raw food ingredients is that they are limited to a few sections of your local farmer's market, co-op, or health foods store. The fruit and produce section, as well as dry goods, will supply you with everything you need, and you're free to forego meat, cheese, dairy, fish, and other processed food sections that generally take up a large percentage of the store. Ideally, you'll be able to limit your sources to a couple of high quality, reliable shops or outlets that are also dedicated to organic whenever possible; shopping then becomes very easy.

All sweeteners are not created equal, and many of us have preferences and opinions on our sweetener of choice. This is never more important than it is in a dessert book.

In raw cooking, we often name agave first, and it was used for most of our recipe testing in this book. Agave has the most neutral flavor of any sweetener and because of that, it is very versatile. When using agave in a recipe, desserts are not always as crisp, which often lends a very pleasant chewy texture to the finished product. This is great for cookies, brownies, and creamy dishes.

In terms of consistency, maple syrup is the most similar to agave, which makes it an easy alternative. Maple syrup has a much more complex, deep flavor and brings its own element to a recipe. If you love maple syrup, it is a great choice, but the maple flavor can be overpowering. Maple syrup is best substituted for agave in chocolate recipes, or recipes with a lot of spice that can stand up to the flavor. Because maple syrup is reduced, the water content is low. When you use it in a dehydrated recipe you won't need to dehydrate the recipe as long; if you do, your recipe may come out slightly crisper (which isn't necessarily a bad thing!). Of course, as natural as it is, maple syrup is not a raw product.

Raw honey is full of incredible properties and flavor, but it is not vegan. Honey is the most difficult substitute because it varies so much in flavor and consistency. However, if you love the flavor of honey it is a great choice. Clover honey is the most common and the most neutral in flavor. Honey is a great substitution in recipes with a lot of fruit and spices. I love honey in chocolate recipes, but it is definitely an acquired taste because the combination creates a very intense flavor.

For hard-to-find ingredients, which we do our best to avoid in this book, there are a large number of excellent internet sources these days, all very reliable and convenient.

I enjoy shopping as much as preparing or eating, simply for the potential it offers—you may be looking for apricots, but stumble upon the most beautiful peaches you've seen in your life—buy them! With food, and especially raw food, nothing is ever set in stone. Be flexible, be local, seasonal, and organic—it's the one way to go, always.

SKILL SET

I do believe that anyone can prepare raw desserts if they carefully read a recipe, take the time to understand the dish they are preparing, and enjoy the process as much as possible. There is nothing dangerous or time sensitive that can throw you off course, no big flames, hot grills or boiling liquids. Rather, it is quite relaxing to actually make a cake with a blender, food processor and a little patience.

In any kitchen, organization is the key to success. In French culinary training, the one term we hear more than any other is "mis en place" or "put in place." It refers to having everything in its proper place, orderly, clean and ready for action. When chopping, soaking, sprouting and otherwise preparing, keep your ingredients in appropriately sized containers, clean and to the side of where you are working.

As far as the act of putting it all together—it is just food. Think about chocolate, relax, enjoy.

raw dessert staples

Once a foundation is established, most food preparation is much easier than it first appears. This is especially true of raw desserts. With an understanding of the more commonly used basics, and by having many of them on hand in your kitchen, you will find that recipes move along much faster and the process is more enjoyable. Here are a few staples you should keep in stock.

coconut milk 14

nut milk or extra creamy nut milk 14

coconut powder 15

sucanat or maple sugar powder 15

chocolate maple glaze 15

nut flour 16

cashew flour 16

irish moss paste 18

date paste 18

candied nuts 20

toffee 20

caramel 21

chocolate chips 21

coconut milk

Our quick version is used for many frostings. For an even richer option, add a bit of mature coconut meat to the Vita-Mix. This is also good as a base for smoothies, with fresh fruit.

1 young Thai coconut

One coconut should yield approximately 2 cups of coconut water and 1 cup of meat. This can vary and will slightly change the thickness of the milk. Blend the water and meat well. The mixture should ideally be the consistency of a heavy cream.

MAKES APPROXIMATELY 3 CUPS

nut milk or extra creamy nut milk

Just as traditional dairy liquids have a variety of forms such as milk, cream, and buttermilk, so do raw ones. The simple distinction is the amount of water used. Four cups water represents an average milky texture, and the less water you use, the thicker and richer the nut milk gets. For these recipes, you want the milk to be more like a heavy cream.

1 cup nuts, soaked 3 to 4 hours, rinsed,
   and drained (almonds, hazelnuts,
   Brazil nuts, or pecans work best)
2½ to 4 cups filtered water

In a Vita-Mix, blend nuts and water until smooth. Squeeze the milk through a cheesecloth or "nut milk" bag. Reserve pulp. Milk stores in the refrigerator for 3 to 4 days.

MAKES APPROXIMATELY 2½ CUPS MILK

coconut powder

This easy-to-prepare staple is light and a good alternative to nut flours.

1 cup shredded coconut

Blend the flakes in a Vita-Mix, using the dry top, to create a light flour.

MAKES APPROXIMATELY 1 CUP

sucanat or maple sugar powder

Sucanat and maple sugar, although not raw, are both minimally processed sweeteners. Sucanat is produced by evaporating cane juice at a very low temperature, so that the water is removed and the result is dark, flavorful granules of sugar. Maple sugar is made by concentrating maple tree sap and grinding it into small crystals. The nature of these sugars makes it difficult to dissolve them, so it is best to powder them in a Vita-Mix before using them in raw food desserts.

1 cup sucanat or maple sugar

Blend in a dry Vita-Mix to make a fine powder.

MAKES 1 CUP

chocolate maple glaze

Rich, smooth, and slightly sweet. Perfect for everything.

1 cup agave nectar, maple syrup, or honey
1 cup cacao powder
2 tablespoons coconut oil, melted

1 teaspoon salt
1 teaspoon vanilla extract

Blend all ingredients until smooth.

MAKES APPROXIMATELY 1 CUP

nut flour

This recipe is best for nuts with skins. An added sustainable fact of preparing raw food is that many of its by-products have excellent uses. Nut milk pulp is a by-product of making nut milk; it actually makes a great flour, which can then be used as a base for cakes, brownies, and other desserts.

After making nut milk (see page 14), place pulp in a thin layer on a Teflex sheet and dehydrate for approximately 24 hours. Once dehydrated, you can process it in the Vita-Mix or food processor to make very light flour. Store in an airtight container.

MAKES APPROXIMATELY 1 CUP FLOUR

cashew flour

Cashews can make instant flour. I use this even for non-raw desserts.

2 cups cashews

In a Vita-Mix with the dry top, quickly powder cashews on high to make a fine flour. You do not want to "blend" the cashews. This flour can be stored in the refrigerator for several weeks.

MAKES APPROXIMATELY 2 CUPS FLOUR

irish moss paste

Irish moss is an invaluable part of contemporary raw dessert preparation, lightening what otherwise may be heavy recipes and acting as a binding agent at the same time.

2 cups soaked moss
½ cup water (use less if possible)

3 to 4 tablespoons agave nectar,
    maple syrup, or honey
1 teaspoon lemon juice

Thoroughly rinse the moss to remove any sand or particles. Soak rinsed moss in cool water for 3 to 4 hours. You do not want to soak it too long because it will decrease its gelling potential.

In a Vita-Mix, blend the moss, adding the water a little at a time. The moss varies in water content, so you may need less. You will create a paste that should be smooth and thick, not watery. Once the desired consistency is achieved, add agave nectar and lemon juice. This makes the perfect Irish moss paste for use in desserts. It will store in the refrigerator for up to 1 week.

MAKES APPROXIMATELY 2 CUPS

date paste

For raw cakes and other cake-like items, it is often preferable to sweeten without adding liquid, which is where date paste is very useful.

1 cup dates, pitted
½ cup water
1 teaspoon lemon juice

In a Vita-Mix, combine all ingredients and blend until smooth. You may want to use more or less water depending on how dry the dates are.

MAKES APPROXIMATELY 1 CUP

candied nuts

Candied nuts are a good pantry item, excellent to add to ice creams or to top other creamy desserts. They make a great snack on their own as well.

4 cups walnuts, pecans, or almonds
1 cup date paste (see page 18)
1 tablespoon vanilla extract
½ tablespoon cinnamon
2 teaspoons sea salt

1 teaspoon powdered ginger
1 teaspoon nutmeg
Pinch cloves
Pinch cayenne

Soak nuts for 4 to 6 hours or overnight in the refrigerator. Rinse well. Combine with remaining ingredients. Dehydrate for at least 24 hours.

MAKES APPROXIMATELY 4 CUPS

toffee

Toffee is great on nearly any ice cream, pudding, or even with fresh fruit.

1 cup coconut oil, melted
1 cup sucanat or maple sugar powder (see page 15)

¼ cup agave nectar, maple syrup, or honey
½ cup chopped almonds

Mix all ingredients in a bowl. This will be a very sweet, sticky mixture. Smooth onto a baking sheet and score into small pieces. Place in freezer until firm. Break into small pieces when ready to use.

MAKES APPROXIMATELY 1½ CUPS TOFFEE PIECES

caramel

This caramel keeps well refrigerated and simply needs to be warmed in the dehydrator prior to serving.

2 cups agave nectar, maple syrup, or honey
1 cup macadamia nuts
¼ cup pine nuts

1 teaspoon vanilla extract
1 teaspoon salt
½ teaspoon lemon juice

Blend all ingredients in a Vita-Mix until smooth.

MAKES APPROXIMATELY 3 CUPS

chocolate chips

Chocolate chips are always necessary!

2 cups cashews
½ cup maple syrup
¼ cup sucanat or maple sugar
   powder (see page 15)

½ cup coconut oil, melted
1 cup cacao powder
½ teaspoon vanilla extract
Pinch salt

MAKES APPROXIMATELY 3 CUPS

Blend all ingredients in a Vita-Mix until smooth. Spread onto a Teflex sheet and dehydrate 6 to 8 hours or overnight. Allow to cool and then break into chips. Keep in refrigerator in a sealed container until ready to use.

cookies and candy

vanilla macaroons 24

raspberry macaroons 26

marzipan 28

pistachio macaroons 30

cacao banana crèmes 31

cardamom cookies 31

chocolate macaroons 32

chocolate-covered pistachio biscotti 34

brigadeiros 36

cacao mint crèmes 38

black-and-white cookies 40

hazelnut butter with chocolate chips 42

blueberry-filled linzer cookies 44

fig newtons 46

vanilla macaroons

This macaroon is lighter, crispier, and more refined than we could have imagined.

1 cup coconut flour
1 cup cashew flour
$\frac{1}{2}$ cup agave powder or powdered sucanat
Pinch salt
3 tablespoons agave nectar, maple syrup, or honey
2 tablespoons water (or more if needed)
$\frac{1}{2}$ teaspoon vanilla extract
1 vanilla bean, scraped

VANILLA CRÈME FILLING
$\frac{1}{2}$ cup macadamia nuts
$\frac{1}{2}$ cup agave nectar, maple syrup, or honey
$\frac{1}{2}$ cup coconut butter, melted
1 vanilla bean, scraped
1 teaspoon vanilla extract
Pinch salt

With a whisk mix dry ingredients. Then add liquid and scraped vanilla bean. You want a doughy consistency that can be easily formed. If you need to add more water, add it a tablespoon at a time. Don't worry about adding too much water; it will evaporate in the dehydrator.

With a small ice cream scoop, scoop about 1 tablespoon of the dough and slightly flatten with your palm. Repeat until all dough is used. Dehydrate 4 to 6 hours. The wetter the dough the longer the macaroons will need to be in the dehydrator. You want them to be crisp on the outside but still chewy on the inside when done.

To make the Vanilla Crème Filling, blend all ingredients until smooth.

Cover half the cookies with vanilla crème filling or a filling flavor of your choice. Put a plain cookie on each covered cookie and press together to make a macaroon cookie sandwich.

MAKES ABOUT 24 SMALL COOKIE HALVES,
12 FILLED MACAROONS

raspberry macaroons

Unlike traditional French macaroons, which are beautiful but utilize food coloring, this version is rendered pink from the natural tint of beet juice. This technique works using almost any vegetable, fruit, or herb juice.

1 cup cashew flour
1 cup coconut flour
1/2 cup agave powder or powdered sucanat
3 tablespoons agave nectar, maple syrup, or honey
2 tablespoons beet juice
1 vanilla bean, scraped
1/2 teaspoon vanilla extract
Pinch salt

RASPBERRY CRÈME FILLING
1/2 cup date paste (see page 18)
1/2 cup fresh raspberries
1 teaspoon lemon juice
1/2 cup coconut butter, melted
1 vanilla bean, scraped
1 teaspoon vanilla extract
Pinch salt

With a whisk mix dry ingredients. Then add liquid. You want a doughy consistency that can be easily formed. If you need to add more water, add it a tablespoon at a time. Don't worry about adding too much water; it will evaporate in the dehydrator.

With a small ice cream scoop, scoop about 1 tablespoon of the dough and slightly flatten with your palm. Repeat until all dough is used. Dehydrate 4 to 6 hours. The wetter the dough the longer the macaroons will need to be in the dehydrator. You want them to be crisp on the outside but still chewy on the inside when done.

To make the raspberry crème filling, blend all ingredients until smooth.

Cover half the cookies with raspberry crème filling or a filling flavor of your choice. Put a plain cookie on each covered cookie and press together to make a macaroon cookie sandwich.

MAKES ABOUT 24 SMALL COOKIE HALVES, 12 FILLED MACAROONS

marzipan

The rose water in this recipe is optional, but it adds an extra floral complexity that is often found in traditional marzipan recipes. The marzipan is great with or without the raspberry jam.

PASTRY
1 cup shredded coconut (powdered in
   Vita-Mix) plus extra for dusting
1/2 cup cashews
1/2 cup macadamia nuts
3/4 cup agave nectar, maple syrup, or honey
1/2 cup agave powder
3 tablespoons almond extract
1 tablespoon rose water
1 tablespoon vanilla extract
Pinch salt
3/4 cup coconut oil, melted

RASPBERRY FILLING
3/4 cup raspberries
1/2 cup date paste (see page 18)
1 tablespoon lemon juice
1 teaspoon vanilla extract
Pinch salt

PASTRY
Make coconut flour in a dry Vita-Mix by blending shredded coconut; blend quickly on high until it is a light, fine flour. Separately, in a clean blender, blend remaining ingredients until smooth adding coconut oil last.

In a food processor combine the coconut flour and the blended mixture; mix well until smooth. Place mixture in the refrigerator until it begins to harden, but is still malleable. Once the mixture is slightly firm, roll into approximately 1/4 inch thick and 1 1/2 inch wide strip.

RASPBERRY FILLING
Blend all ingredients until smooth. Dehydrate for 5 to 6 hours until the jam becomes very thick.

ASSEMBLY
Spread a thin layer of the raspberry jam in the center of the strip. Roll strip into a log. Dust with coconut flour. Store in the refrigerator until it is firm. Slice into medallions for serving.

MAKES ABOUT 2 DOZEN SMALL PIECES

pistachio macaroons

This is one of my personal favorites. And, like the raspberry macaroon, this recipe is a great example of natural food coloring.

1 cup cashew flour
1 cup coconut flour
½ cup agave powder or powdered sucanat
3 tablespoons agave nectar, maple syrup, or honey
2 tablespoons spinach juice
1 vanilla bean, scraped
½ teaspoon vanilla extract
Pinch salt

PISTACHIO CRÈME FILLING
½ cup pistachios
½ cup agave nectar, maple syrup, or honey
½ cup coconut butter, melted
1 vanilla bean, scraped
1 teaspoon vanilla extract
Pinch salt

With a whisk mix dry ingredients. Then add liquid. You want a doughy consistency that can be easily formed. If you need to add more water, add it a tablespoon at a time. Don't worry about adding too much water; it will evaporate in the dehydrator.

With a small ice cream scoop, scoop about 1 tablespoon of the dough and slightly flatten with your palm. Repeat until all dough is used. Dehydrate 4 to 6 hours. The wetter the dough the longer the macaroons will need to be in the dehydrator. You want them to be crisp on the outside but still chewy on the inside when done.

To make the pistachio crème filling, blend all ingredients until smooth.

Cover half the cookies with pistachio crème filling or a filling flavor of your choice. Put a plain cookie on each covered cookie and press together to make a macaroon cookie sandwich.

MAKES ABOUT 24 SMALL COOKIE HALVES, 12 FILLED MACAROONS

cacao banana crèmes

Chocolate, banana, and crème—enough said. Universal appeal.

1 cup shredded coconut
1 cup cashews
1 cup mashed bananas
¾ cup agave nectar, maple syrup, or honey
¼ cup cacao powder

1 tablespoon vanilla extract
1 teaspoon lemon juice
Pinch salt
¾ cup coconut oil, melted
1 cup chocolate maple glaze (see page 15)

Make coconut flour in a dry Vita-Mix by blending shredded coconut; blend quickly on high until it is a light, fine flour. Separately, in a clean blender, blend remaining ingredients except glaze until smooth adding coconut oil last.

In a food processor combine the coconut flour and the blended mixture; mix well until smooth. Place mixture in the refrigerator until it begins to harden, but is still malleable. Once the mixture is slightly firm, roll into a log and slice into medallions. Refrigerate medallions until very firm and then dip in chocolate maple glaze coating. Store in the refrigerator.

MAKES 1 DOZEN LARGE PATTIES, 2 DOZEN SMALL

cardamom cookies

Cardamom is a savory spice that is particularly well suited to desserts that use coconut and almond.

3 cups shredded coconut
2 cups almond flour
1 cup agave nectar, maple syrup, or honey
1 tablespoon vanilla extract
1 teaspoon almond extract

1 vanilla bean, scraped
½ tablespoon cardamom powder
1 teaspoon salt
½ cup coconut oil, melted
36 almonds for garnish

In a food processor combine the shredded coconut and almond flour. Process until well combined. Add the remaining ingredients and process into dough. Scoop cookies with a tablespoon or small ice cream scoop, making small 1 to 1½-inch cookies. Press an almond into each cookie. Dehydrate for at least 24 hours.

MAKES ABOUT 3 DOZEN COOKIES

chocolate macaroons

Simply delicious.

1 cup cashew flour
½ cup coconut flour
½ cup cacao powder
½ cup agave powder or powdered sucanat
3 tablespoons agave nectar, maple syrup, or honey
2 tablespoons water
1 vanilla bean, scraped
½ teaspoon vanilla extract
Pinch salt

CHOCOLATE CRÈME FILLING
½ cup macadamia nuts
¼ cup cacao powder
½ cup agave nectar, maple syrup, or honey
½ cup coconut butter, melted
1 vanilla bean, scraped
1 teaspoon vanilla extract
Pinch salt

With a whisk mix dry ingredients. Then add liquid. You want a doughy consistency that can be easily formed. If you need to add more water, add it a tablespoon at a time. Don't worry about adding too much water; it will evaporate in the dehydrator.

With a small ice cream scoop, scoop about 1 tablespoon of the dough and slightly flatten with your palm. Repeat until all dough is used. Dehydrate 4 to 6 hours. The wetter the dough the longer the macaroons will need to be in the dehydrator. You want them to be crisp on the outside but still chewy on the inside when done.

To make the chocolate crème filling, blend all ingredients until smooth.

Cover half the cookies with chocolate crème filling or a filling flavor of your choice. Put a plain cookie on each covered cookie and press together to make a macaroon cookie sandwich.

**MAKES ABOUT 24 SMALL COOKIE HALVES,
12 FILLED MACAROONS**

chocolate-covered pistachio biscotti

Biscotti is one of my favorite things for breakfast, and, with the addition of chocolate, this version is also perfect for dessert.

2 cups almond flour
1 cup pistachio flour*
1/2 cup coarsely chopped pistachios
2 tablespoons flax meal
2 tablespoons agave nectar, maple syrup, or honey
2 tablespoons water
1 teaspoon cinnamon
1 teaspoon almond extract

1 tablespoon vanilla extract
1/4 cup orange juice (or more if needed)
1 tablespoon orange zest
1 cup chocolate maple glaze (see page 15)

*Lightly pulse pistachios in dry
  Vita-Mix to make flour.

In a food processor combine all ingredients until well mixed. Remove and form a dough-like ball. If the mixture is too dry add a few extra tablespoons of orange juice or water.

Form a rectangular log approximately 1 inch tall. Slice into ¾-inch slices. For longer biscotti, slice on the diagonal; for shorter, cut straight. Dehydrate for at least 24 hours.

NOTE: You cannot overdehydrate—you want the biscotti to be very firm and crisp. These will keep for months in the refrigerator.

When ready to serve, dip in chocolate maple glaze and place in the refrigerator until firm.

MAKES ABOUT 12 BISCOTTI

brigadeiros

Brazilian truffles, *brigadeiros,* are fun, textural, and decadent—the Carmen Miranda of truffles.

¾ cup raw cacao powder
1½ cups cashews, soaked 2 to 4 hours
¾ cup agave nectar, maple syrup, or honey
1 teaspoon vanilla extract

1 teaspoon cinnamon
½ teaspoon salt
¾ cup cacao butter, melted
Approximately 1 cup cacao nibs

Blend all ingredients except for the cacao butter and cacao nibs in a Vita-Mix until smooth. Slowly add the cacao butter and continue to blend until completely incorporated. Pour into a bowl and place in the refrigerator for 15 to 30 minutes until mixture becomes firm enough to scoop and mold. Using a small ice cream scoop make balls, about 2 teaspoons in size. Roll in cacao nibs to coat.

MAKES ABOUT 2 DOZEN TRUFFLES

cacao mint crèmes

Perfectly decadent and refreshing, this version of mint crèmes is very similar to a traditional peppermint pattie but without all of the refined sugar.

1 cup shredded coconut
1 cup cashews
1/2 cup macadamia nuts
2/3 cup agave nectar, maple syrup, or honey
1/4 cup mint leaves, ribs and stems removed
2 teaspoons peppermint extract

1 teaspoon vanilla extract
1 teaspoon lemon juice
Pinch salt
1/2 cup coconut oil, melted
1 cup chocolate maple glaze (see page 15)

Make coconut flour in a dry Vita-Mix using shredded coconut; blend quickly on high until it is a light, fine flour. Separately, in a clean blender, blend remaining ingredients except chocolate maple glaze until smooth, adding coconut oil last.

In a food processor combine the coconut flour and the blended mixture; mix well until smooth. Place mixture in the refrigerator until it begins to harden, but is still malleable. Once the mixture is slightly firm roll into a log and slice into medallions. Refrigerate medallions until very firm and then dip in chocolate maple glaze coating. Store in the refrigerator.

MAKES 1 DOZEN LARGE PATTIES, 2 DOZEN SMALL

black-and-white cookies

Dramatic to the eye, the black-and-white cookie is a New York City favorite. The styling of this cookie is often underestimated, but makes for great presentation.

3 cups cashew flour
1 cup macadamia nuts (powdered in Vita-Mix)
2 cups coconut flour
¾ cup agave nectar, maple syrup, or honey
1 to 2 tablespoons coconut oil, melted
2 tablespoons vanilla extract
½ teaspoon salt
Water (if needed)
½ cup chocolate maple glaze (see page 15)

COCONUT GLAZE
½ cup young coconut meat
¼ cup agave nectar, maple syrup, or honey
1 tablespoon coconut oil, melted
½ teaspoon vanilla extract
½ teaspoon salt

In a food processor mix the cashew, macadamia nut, and coconut flours until well combined. Then add the remaining ingredients, except glazes, and process until a dough is formed. You may need to add a few tablespoons of water in order to make the mixture soft enough to work with.

With a rolling pin, roll out dough to be approximately ½ inch thick. Using a round cookie cutter, cut into perfect circles. Dehydrate for 8 to 12 hours or overnight.

To make the coconut glaze, blend all ingredients in a Vita-Mix until smooth.

Frost or dip cookies, half with chocolate maple glaze and half with coconut glaze.

MAKES ABOUT 12 COOKIES

hazelnut butter with chocolate chips

This recipe works well with any nut butter you may prefer. As you might notice throughout this book, I just happen to love the combination of hazelnut with chocolate.

2 cups almond flour
1 cup hazelnut flour
¼ cup flax meal
½ cup raw hazelnut butter
1 cup agave nectar, maple syrup, or honey

¼ cup sucanat or maple sugar powder (see page 15)
2 teaspoons salt
6 tablespoons vanilla extract
Water (if needed)
1 cup cacao nibs, ¼ cup reserved for topping

Combine all ingredients except for nibs or chocolate chips in food processor. If the dough is too dry add a few tablespoons of water. Mix in the nibs or chocolate chips. Form into 3-inch cookies.

Press remaining chocolate chips on the top. Dehydrate for at least 24 hours.

MAKES 24 COOKIES

blueberry-filled linzer cookies

Traditionally made with blanched almonds and black currant preserves, this is our Maine blueberry version of the linzer cookie. Feel free to use any berries that you would like.

PASTRY
3 cups almond flour
2 cups coconut flour, divided
¾ cup agave nectar, maple syrup, or honey
1 tablespoon lemon zest
1 to 2 tablespoons coconut oil, melted
2 tablespoons vanilla extract
½ teaspoon salt

BLUEBERRY JAM
¾ cup blueberries
½ cup date paste (see page 18)
1 tablespoon lemon juice
1 teaspoon vanilla extract
Pinch salt

PASTRY

In a food processor mix the almond flour and 1½ cups of the coconut flour until well combined. Then add the remaining ingredients and process until dough is formed. You may need to add a few tablespoons of water in order to make the mixture soft enough to work with.

With a rolling pin, roll out dough to be approximately ¼ inch thick—you want the dough to be thin. Using a linzer cookie cutter, cut into linzer shapes, making an even amount of cookies. Cut half of the cookies with a circular cutout and half without. Dehydrate for 10 to 12 hours or until the cookies are very crisp.

BLUEBERRY JAM

Blend all ingredients until smooth. Place in the dehydrator for 2 to 3 hours until jam becomes slightly thick.

ASSEMBLY

Spread about 1 tablespoon blueberry jam on a solid cookie and top with a cutout cookie to make a sandwich. Dust with reserved coconut flour.

MAKES APPROXIMATELY 1 DOZEN COOKIES

fig newtons

Everyone is familiar with the traditional Fig Newton—white flour pastry filled with fig jam. This is our version. Feel free to experiment with different dried fruits if figs aren't your favorite.

PASTRY
4 cups cashew flour
1 cup almond flour
1/2 cup macadamia nuts
1 cup agave nectar, maple syrup, or honey
2 tablespoons vanilla extract
1 teaspoon salt
1 tablespoon coconut oil, melted

PASTRY
In a food processor mix all pastry ingredients until smooth to make a dough. Divide the dough in half and form two identical 1/2-inch rectangles. (You will eventually be stacking them on top of one another.) Dehydrate for 3 to 6 hours until the dough is slightly firm, but still malleable.

FILLING
In a Vita-Mix blend all ingredients until smooth.

FILLING
2 cups dried figs, soaked to soften
1/2 cup agave nectar, maple syrup, or honey
1 tablespoon lemon juice
1 tablespoon orange zest
Pinch salt
Splash of water if needed to blend

ASSEMBLY
Spread filling on top of one of the rectangular cookies, leaving about 1/4 inch on each side. Place the other cookie on top. The dough should still be malleable enough to connect the sides to create the traditional Fig Newton shape. Slice the log into approximately 24 cookies. Place in the dehydrator without Teflex and dehydrate for 12 hours or more, until cookies are firm, but chewy.

MAKES ABOUT 2 DOZEN COOKIES

brownies, bars, and fudge

midnight fudge brownie 50

chocolate hazelnut fudge 51

cherry cacao bars 51

rocky road brownies 52

chocolate-apricot orange bars with praline 54

blondies 55

hello dollies 55

raspberry streusel bars 56

white chocolate cheesecake brownies 58

pecan divinity fudge 59

baklava 60

gianduja 62

midnight fudge brownie

Aptly named for its service as a midnight snack or the fact that it may keep you up well past that hour.

WET INGREDIENTS

1 cup cacao powder
½ cup macadamia nuts
1 cup cashews
1 cup water
¼ cup date paste (see page 18)
¼ cup agave nectar, maple syrup, or honey
1 teaspoon lemon juice
1 teaspoon salt

DRY INGREDIENTS

2 cups cashew flour
2 cups Brazil nut flour
1 cup cacao powder
2 teaspoons salt
1 tablespoon vanilla extract

MAPLE GLAZE

½ cup maple syrup, agave nectar, or honey
½ cup cacao powder
1 teaspoon salt
1 teaspoon vanilla extract

Blend all wet ingredients except cacao powder until smooth in a Vita-Mix. Then slowly add cacao powder.

Mix all dry ingredients well in a food processor or mixer and then combine with the wet ingredients.

Press into a brownie pan (preferably with a removable bottom) and place into the dehydrator for 2 to 3 hours until firm. Spread on the maple glaze. Then remove from pan and dehydrate overnight on plane rack 10 to 12 hours more.

MAKES 24 SMALLER SQUARES, 16 BIG SQUARES

chocolate hazelnut fudge

Chocolate with hazelnuts is often referred to as *gianduja* in Italy, where it can frequently be found in gelato.

½ cup coconut butter
½ cup cacao butter
1 cup hazelnut butter
2 teaspoons vanilla extract

1 cup agave nectar, maple syrup, or honey
1 cup cacao powder
1 teaspoon salt

Blend all ingredients in a Vita-Mix until smooth. Pour into brownie pan and refrigerate.

MAKES 24 SMALL FUDGE PIECES

cherry cacao bars

This is another recipe that would be great as a breakfast or snack—it's not overly sweet and it's easy to store.

4 cups almond flour
3 cups cashew flour
1 cup dried cherries, chopped
½ cup cacao nibs
½ cup cacao powder
¼ cup flax meal

1½ cups agave nectar, maple syrup, or honey
2 teaspoons sea salt
1 tablespoon vanilla extract
1 tablespoon orange zest (optional)
1 tablespoon orange juice
½ cup chocolate maple glaze (see page 15)

Mix all dry ingredients together in a large mixing bowl. Then add agave and remaining ingredients except maple glaze. Mix thoroughly. Spread evenly on a parchment-lined half sheet pan and press firmly. Dehydrate overnight.

Turn onto a cutting board and cut into rectangular bars. Return to the dehydrator for another 1 to 2 hours. Spread with chocolate maple glaze if desired.

MAKES APPROXIMATELY 24 BARS

rocky road brownies

If you are unable to source marshmallow extract, don't worry about it. The recipe works well with or without it.

WET INGREDIENTS

½ cup macadamia nuts
1 cup cashews
1 cup water
¼ cup date paste (see page 18)
¼ cup agave nectar, maple syrup, or honey
1 teaspoon lemon juice
1 teaspoon salt
1 cup cacao powder

DRY INGREDIENTS

2 cups cashew flour
2 cups Brazil nut flour
1 cup cacao powder
2 teaspoons salt
1 tablespoon vanilla extract

MARSHMALLOW CRÈME

1 cup cashews, soaked
¾ cup agave nectar, maple syrup, or honey
¼ cup coconut oil, melted
2 teaspoons vanilla extract
¼ teaspoon salt
1 bottle marshmallow extract

TOPPINGS

1 cup caramel (see page 21)
½ cup chocolate maple glaze (see page 15)
1 cup candied nuts (see page 20)

BROWNIE

Blend all wet ingredients except cacao powder until smooth in a Vita-Mix. Then slowly add cacao powder.

Mix all dry ingredients well in a food processor or mixer and then combine with the wet ingredients.

Press into a brownie pan (preferably with a removable bottom) and place in the dehydrator for 2 to 3 hours until firm. Then remove from pan and dehydrate overnight on plane rack 10 to 12 hours more.

MARSHMALLOW CRÈME

Blend all ingredients until smooth. Store in the refrigerator until ready to use.

ASSEMBLY

Smooth marshmallow crème on top of dehydrated brownie. Top with chopped caramel, chocolate maple glaze, and chopped candied nuts when ready to serve.

MAKES 24 SMALLER SQUARES, 16 BIG SQUARES

chocolate-apricot orange bars with praline

Feel free to try this with another dried fruit. Pear and mango are good options.

BARS

4 cups almond flour
3 cups cashew flour
1 cup dried apricots, chopped
½ cup cacao powder
¼ cup flax meal
1½ cups agave nectar, maple syrup, or honey
½ cup chopped orange, seeds and
  membranes removed

2 teaspoons sea salt
1 tablespoon vanilla extract
1 tablespoon orange zest (optional)
1 tablespoon orange juice

TOPPING

1 cup caramel (see page 21)
¼ cup chopped almonds

Mix all dry ingredients together in a large mixing bowl. Then blend agave nectar and remaining ingredients in Vita-Mix until smooth. Add agave mixture to dry mixture and mix thoroughly. Spread evenly on a parchment-lined half sheet pan and press firmly. Dehydrate overnight.

Turn onto a cutting board and cut into rectangular bars. Return to the dehydrator for another 1 to 2 hours.

For topping, mix caramel and chopped almonds to make praline. Frost bars with praline mixture.

MAKES APPROXIMATELY 24 BARS

blondies

Traditional blondies are flavored with brown sugar—sucanat is very similar in taste and also provides the caramel color that blondies are known for.

WET INGREDIENTS

1 cup cashews
1/2 cup macadamia nuts
1/4 cup water
3/4 cup agave nectar, maple syrup, or honey
1 teaspoon lemon juice
1 tablespoon vanilla extract
2 teaspoons salt

DRY INGREDIENTS

2 cups cashew flour
1 cup almond flour
1 cup coconut flour
1/4 cup sucanat or maple sugar
   powder (see page 15)

Blend all wet ingredients until smooth in a Vita-Mix.

Mix all dry ingredients well in a food processor and then combine with the wet ingredients.

Press into a brownie pan (preferably with a removable bottom) and place into the dehydrator for 2 to 3 hours until firm. Then remove from pan and dehydrate overnight on dehydrator tray 10 to 12 hours more.

MAKES APPROXIMATELY 12 BARS

hello dollies

Cacao nibs are often preferred over raw cacao chips if the dish in which they are included is already sweet.

CRUST

3 cups cashew flour
4 tablespoons agave nectar, maple syrup, or honey
1 tablespoon coconut oil, melted
Pinch sea salt

FILLING

1 cup chopped walnuts
1 cup cacao nibs
1 1/2 cups shredded coconut
1 cup agave nectar, maple syrup, or honey
1 teaspoon vanilla extract
1 teaspoon sea salt

In a mixing bowl mix together all ingredients for crust. Press into a 9-inch brownie pan.

Mix together walnuts, nibs, and shredded coconut then add agave, vanilla, and salt. This should be a very sticky mixture. Spread on top of the crust. Place in the dehydrator for 3 to 4 hours so that it becomes slightly warm and chewy.

MAKES 12 BARS

raspberry streusel bars

For a meeting, afternoon tea, or coffee, these are ideal.

CRUST

3 cups cashew flour
4 tablespoons agave nectar, maple syrup, or honey
1 tablespoon coconut oil, melted
Pinch sea salt

FILLING

3 cups fresh or frozen raspberries
1/2 cup agave nectar, maple syrup, or honey
1/4 cup Irish moss paste (see page 18)
1 tablespoon lemon juice
1 teaspoon vanilla extract
1/2 teaspoon sea salt

STREUSEL

1 cup pecans
1/4 cup sucanat or maple sugar
   powder (see page 15)
1 teaspoon cinnamon
1 teaspoon vanilla extract
1 teaspoon salt

GLAZE

1/2 cup cashews
1/2 cup young coconut meat
1/2 cup agave nectar, maple syrup, or honey
1/4 cup water
3 tablespoons coconut oil, melted
1 teaspoon vanilla extract
Pinch salt

In a mixing bowl, mix the ingredients for the crust. Press into a brownie or terrine pan with a removable bottom. (If you do not have a pan with a removable bottom, line the pan with plastic wrap so that you can easily remove the bars.)

To make the filling, blend all ingredients in a Vita-Mix until smooth. To make the streusel, pulse ingredients in a food processor until chunky. For the glaze, blend all ingredients in a Vita-Mix until smooth.

Pour raspberry filling on top of crust and sprinkle with streusel topping. Dehydrate for 6 to 8 hours, or longer if you want a chewier bar. Once bars are dehydrated, drizzle with glaze.

MAKES ABOUT 12 BARS

white chocolate cheesecake brownies

Any variation of cheesecake filling works well on this brownie base.

BROWNIES

4 cups cashew flour
4 cups cacao powder
1 1/2 cups agave nectar, maple syrup, or honey
1/2 cup coconut oil, melted
1 tablespoon vanilla extract
1 teaspoon cinnamon
1 teaspoon salt

CHEESECAKE

1/2 cup dates
1/2 cup agave nectar, maple syrup, or honey
1/2 cup lemon juice
1 vanilla bean, scraped
1 teaspoon salt
2 cups cashews
1/2 cup young coconut meat
1/2 cup cacao butter, melted

In a food processor combine cashew flour and cacao powder. Then add remaining ingredients until well combined. Be careful not to overblend. Press into a 9-inch brownie pan with a removable bottom and dehydrate for 24 hours.

Blend dates, agave, lemon juice, vanilla, and salt in a Vita-Mix until smooth. Then add the cashews and coconut meat and continue to blend until smooth. Add the cacao butter last.

Pour cheesecake layer over dehydrated brownie layer and place in the refrigerator until firm.

MAKES 12 BARS

pecan divinity fudge

Meredith tells me that divinity fudge was one of her favorite Southern sweets to buy at pecan farms in Georgia. It is traditionally made with egg whites and corn syrup. Although I've never experienced the original version, I can't imagine this one is missing anything.

1 cup shredded coconut
1 cup cashews
1/2 cup macadamia nuts
2/3 cup agave nectar, maple syrup, or honey
1 tablespoon vanilla extract

1 teaspoon lemon juice
Pinch salt
3/4 cup coconut butter, melted
1/2 cup chopped pecans

Make coconut flour in a dry Vita-Mix using shredded coconut; blend quickly on high until it is a light, fine flour. Separately, in a clean blender, blend all remaining ingredients except for the pecans. Blend until smooth, adding coconut butter last.

In a food processor combine the coconut flour (reserving 1/4 cup) and the blended mixture; mix well until smooth. Mix in the chopped pecans.

Place mixture in the refrigerator until it begins to harden, but is still malleable. Once the mixture is doughlike in consistency, make into balls approximately 2 tablespoons in size and roll in reserved 1/4 cup coconut flour. Store in the refrigerator.

MAKES ABOUT 24 PIECES

baklava

The phyllo dough used here is also excellent to layer with a custard recipe, such as that in dulce de leche, to create a sort of mille-feuille.

PHYLLO DOUGH

1½ cups cashews
1½ cups macadamia nuts
3 tablespoons lemon juice
4 tablespoons raw honey
1 cup water
2 tablespoons vanilla extract
1 teaspoon salt
2 tablespoons flax meal

FILLING

3 cups walnuts, soaked and dehydrated
2 teaspoons cinnamon
1 teaspoon nutmeg
½ teaspoon cardamom
¼ teaspoon cloves
¼ teaspoon ginger
1 teaspoon salt
½ cup raw honey

To make the phyllo, blend all ingredients in a Vita-Mix except flax meal until smooth. Then add flax meal and continue to blend. Spread mixture thinly on dehydrator sheet lined with Teflex. Dehydrate for 6 to 8 hours or overnight at 115 degrees F. You do not want it to be crumbly. If it does get too dehydrated to remove from Teflex you can rehydrate by brushing it with a little water.

To make the filling, lightly process the walnuts and dry ingredients. Mix in the honey. Layer the phyllo and the walnut filling. Before serving brush with honey or agave.

MAKES ABOUT 12 SERVINGS

gianduja

Hazelnut and chocolate: the perfect marriage.

1 cup cacao butter, melted
2 vanilla beans, scraped
1 teaspoon hazelnut extract
½ teaspoon salt

1 cup agave nectar, maple syrup, or honey
1 cup cacao powder
½ cup raw hazelnut butter
1 cup coarsely chopped hazelnuts

Blend cacao butter, vanilla beans, hazelnut extract, and salt in a Vita-Mix until smooth. Then add the agave nectar, cacao powder, and hazelnut butter; blend until completely combined. Pour into a large mixing bowl and stir in the chopped hazelnuts.

Lightly oil a 9-inch pan (preferably with a removable bottom). Pour in mixture. Store in the refrigerator to set.

MAKES ABOUT 12 PIECES

puddings, flans, and custards

green tea flan

Most sushi aficionados know how good green tea ice cream can taste after a salty meal. It has the same effect after a raw meal, offering sweetness but in a very subtle form.

1 cup cashews
1 cup young coconut meat
1/2 cup agave nectar, maple syrup, or honey
2/3 cup coconut oil, melted
1/4 cup Irish moss paste (see page 18)

2 tablespoons matcha (powdered Japanese green tea)
1 teaspoon lemon juice
1/4 teaspoon salt
1 vanilla bean, scraped

Blend cashews, coconut meat, and agave nectar in a Vita-Mix until smooth. Add all other ingredients and continue to blend until smooth. Do not overblend. Pour into a flan mold or any smooth-sided ramekin and refrigerate for 2 hours or longer until set.

MAKES 4 TO 6 SERVINGS

butterscotch pudding

Butterscotch reminds most of us of childhood. It's perfect for adulthood moments when we're craving the classics.

2 cups young coconut meat
1 cup macadamia nuts
2/3 cup cashews
1/4 cup pine nuts
1 cup agave nectar, maple syrup, or honey

1 tablespoon vanilla extract
1/2 tablespoon organic butterscotch extract
1/2 tablespoon salt
1/4 cup coconut oil, melted

Blend all ingredients in a Vita-Mix until smooth.

MAKES 4 TO 6 SERVINGS

bitter orange crème caramel

Whereas the juice from an orange is one-dimensional, the peel provides the flavor I prefer. It may be dehydrated and used in powder form for added intensity, candied, or simply used in its fresh form as zest such as it is here.

FLAN
1 cup young coconut meat
1 cup cashews
½ cup Irish moss paste (see page 18)
½ cup fresh squeezed orange juice
¾ cup agave nectar, maple syrup, or honey
⅔ cup coconut oil, melted
1 tablespoon lemon juice
1 teaspoon orange extract

½ teaspoon salt
2 tablespoons orange zest
1 vanilla bean, scraped

TOPPING
6 to 8 tablespoons agave nectar,
   maple syrup, or honey

2 tablespoons orange zest

Blend coconut meat, cashews, Irish moss paste, orange juice, and agave nectar in a Vita-Mix until smooth. Gradually add coconut oil and remaining five ingredients for flan; continue to blend until smooth. Pour into a flan mold or any smooth-sided ramekin and refrigerate for 2 hours or longer until set. When firm, turn over and remove from ramekin.

Mix agave nectar and orange zest. After plated, drizzle each dish with maple-orange topping.

MAKES 6 TO 8 SERVINGS

dulce de leche flan

Translated from Spanish as "sweet milk," *dulce de leche* often uses canned condensed milk, which is tasty but pretty far removed from nature. This recipe uses agave nectar, which provides a bit of caramel essence that gives an added layer of flavor.

½ cup cashews
1 cup young coconut meat
½ cup agave nectar, maple syrup, or honey
½ cup macadamia nuts
⅔ cup coconut oil, melted
¼ cup Irish moss paste (see page 18)

1 teaspoon lemon juice
¼ teaspoon salt
2 vanilla beans, scraped
1 teaspoon vanilla extract
6 to 8 tablespoons agave nectar,
   maple syrup, or honey

Blend cashews, coconut meat, and agave nectar in a Vita-Mix until smooth. Add all other ingredients except agave for serving and continue to blend until smooth. Do not overblend. Pour into a flan mold or any smooth-sided ramekin and refrigerate for 2 hours or longer until set. When firm, turn over and remove from ramekin. After plated, drizzle each dish with approximately 2 tablespoons agave nectar.

MAKES 6 SERVINGS

white chocolate mousse

This is the true white chocolate—the oil of raw cacao beans has a distinct flavor without the dark chocolate intensity, making it well-suited for refined but subtle recipes.

1 cup cashews
1 cup young coconut meat
¼ cup Irish moss paste (see page 18)
½ cup light agave nectar, maple syrup, or honey

½ cup cacao oil, melted
2 teaspoons vanilla extract
2 vanilla beans, scraped
¼ teaspoon salt

Blend all ingredients in a Vita-Mix until smooth.

MAKES 6 TO 8 SERVINGS

chai chia pudding

Hands down, one of the best comfort food desserts! Chia seeds are the perfect nutrient-packed replacement for tapioca—they can soak up ten times their weight in water.

1 cup cashews
2 cups water
½ cup honey
1 tablespoon cinnamon
¼ teaspoon nutmeg

¼ teaspoon ginger
1 teaspoon vanilla extract
1 vanilla bean, scraped
¼ teaspoon salt
½ cup chia seeds

Blend all ingredients except for the chia seeds in a Vita-Mix until smooth, making a cashew crème. Pour crème over chia seeds and allow to soak for 2 hours or more until the chia becomes a tapioca consistency.

VARIATION: Add fresh fruit or dried fruit and nuts to your liking for a delicious breakfast.

MAKES 4 SERVINGS

bavarian crème

I have always loved the idea of Bavarian Crème, but never the reality of what was in it. Until now.

1 cup cashews
1 cup young coconut meat
1/2 cup macadamia nuts
1/4 cup Irish moss paste (see page 18)
3/4 cup agave nectar, maple syrup, or honey

2 to 3 vanilla beans, scraped
1/4 cup coconut oil, melted
1 tablespoon lemon juice
1/4 teaspoon salt

Blend the first six ingredients in a Vita-Mix until smooth. Add coconut oil, lemon juice, and salt and finish blending until smooth. Make sure that you do not overblend the oil.

MAKES 6 TO 8 SERVINGS

orange blossom honey pudding

Orange blossoms are intoxicating, whether they are flavoring food, a perfume, or the fresh air. If orange blossom honey is not available, a couple of drops of orange extract added to regular honey will achieve similar results.

1 cup young coconut meat
1 cup cashews
1/2 cup fresh squeezed orange juice
1/4 cup apple juice or water
3/4 cup raw orange blossom honey
2/3 cup coconut oil, melted

1 tablespoon lemon juice
1/2 teaspoon salt
2 tablespoons orange zest
1 vanilla bean, scraped
1 teaspoon salt

Blend first five ingredients in a Vita-Mix until smooth. Then add remaining ingredients and blend until smooth.

MAKES 6 TO 8 SERVINGS

double chocolate pudding

This is similar to other raw chocolate pudding recipes, but has the unusual addition of cacao oil, adding a layer of complexity.

1 cup cashews
¾ cup young coconut meat
¾ cup agave nectar, maple syrup, or honey
6 tablespoons cacao oil, melted

6 tablespoons coconut oil, melted
1 cup cocoa powder
1 teaspoon vanilla extract
¼ teaspoon salt

Blend first three ingredients in a Vita-Mix until smooth. Add remaining ingredients and continue to blend until smooth.

MAKES 6 TO 8 SERVINGS

milk chocolate pudding

You must try it! Avocados and dessert are better suited than you can imagine.

2 avocados, pitted and peeled
1 cup almond milk (or any nut milk)
¾ cup agave nectar, maple syrup, or honey
¾ cup cocoa powder

1 teaspoon vanilla extract
¼ teaspoon cinnamon
Pinch salt

Blend all ingredients in a Vita-Mix until smooth.

MAKES 4 TO 6 SERVINGS

vanilla-almond panna cotta with fig compote

This is even better with fresh figs—green or black—if they are in season.

PANNA COTTA
3 cups cashews
1/2 cup young coconut meat
1 1/2 cups raw agave nectar, maple syrup, or honey
2 cups almond milk
1/4 cup Irish moss paste (see page 18)
2 tablespoons vanilla extract
1/2 cup coconut oil, melted
1 tablespoon vanilla extract
2 teaspoons almond extract
1 vanilla bean, scraped

1 tablespoon lemon juice
1/4 teaspoon salt

FIG COMPOTE
1 cup dried figs
1/2 cup agave nectar, maple syrup, or honey
2 teaspoons cinnamon
1 teaspoon nutmeg
2 tablespoons orange juice
Pinch salt

To make panna cotta, blend first six ingredients in a Vita-Mix until smooth. Then add the coconut oil and remaining ingredients and blend until smooth. Freeze in custard molds until ready to use.

To make fig compote, soak figs in water 30 minutes or until soft. Drain. Then blend in a Vita-Mix or food processor with remaining ingredients.

Do not overblend; leave compote as a chunky texture.

Remove panna cotta from molds and serve each with a generous dollop of fig compote.

MAKES 6 TO 8 SERVINGS

pies and tarts

banana crème pie

I've always thought of banana crème as the flavor used for pie throwing, but I can't imagine not wanting to eat this!

CRUST
1½ cups macadamia nuts
½ cup shredded coconut
½ teaspoon salt
3 tablespoons agave nectar, maple syrup, or honey
1 tablespoon coconut oil, melted
1 teaspoon vanilla extract

BANANA CRÈME FILLING
3 cups soaked cashews
2 cups mashed banana
1 cup agave nectar, maple syrup, or honey
2 teaspoons vanilla extract
1 tablespoon lemon juice
¼ teaspoon salt
½ cup coconut oil, melted

COCONUT CRÈME
1½ cups soaked cashews
1½ cups coconut milk (see page 14)
½ cup agave nectar, maple syrup, or honey
1 tablespoon vanilla extract
1 teaspoon lemon juice
1 cup coconut oil, melted
Pinch salt
1 sliced banana for layering

To make the crust, in a food processor blend the macadamia nuts, shredded coconut, and salt until they become crumbly flour. Add the agave nectar, coconut oil, and vanilla; lightly pulse until all ingredients are well mixed but only stick together when pressed between your fingers.

To make the banana crème filling, blend all the ingredients except the coconut oil in a Vita-Mix until smooth. Add the coconut oil and blend until combined.

To make the coconut crème, blend the first five ingredients in a Vita-Mix until smooth. Then add coconut oil and salt and continue to blend until completely combined. Put in the refrigerator for a few minutes so it can set.

To assemble, press crust into a 9-inch tart pan with a removable bottom. Pour in banana crème filling. Top with banana slices. Top with coconut crème. Let set in the refrigerator for at least 30 minutes before serving.

MAKES 1 (9-INCH) PIE

white peach tart

The white peach embodies warm weather. This is a great dessert to follow a light summer meal or to enjoy with a cold sparkling wine.

CRUST
1 cup almonds, soaked overnight and dehydrated
1¼ cups cashews
3 tablespoons agave nectar, maple syrup, or honey
1 tablespoon coconut oil, melted
¼ teaspoon salt

FILLING
3 cups cashews, soaked 1 to 2 hours
½ cup peeled and sliced white peaches
¼ cup lemon juice

¾ cup agave nectar, maple syrup, or honey
1 tablespoon vanilla extract
1 teaspoon cinnamon
1 teaspoon salt
1 vanilla bean, scraped
¾ cup coconut oil, melted

TOPPING
2 cups sliced white peaches
¼ cup agave nectar, maple syrup, or honey
1 tablespoon lemon juice

To make the crust, place prepared almonds and cashews in a food processor and pulse into a coarse flour. Add remaining ingredients and lightly pulse until well mixed. Press into a 9-inch tart pan with a removable bottom.

To make the filling, blend all ingredients except coconut oil in a Vita-Mix until smooth.

Then add the coconut oil and blend until completely combined, but do not overblend.

To make the fruit topping, toss sliced peaches with agave and lemon juice. Pour filling into crust and arrange sliced fruit on top.

MAKES 1 (9-INCH) TART

chocolate walnut tart

Walnuts are not used in raw food as frequently as cashews and almonds, but their texture and richness work well with other deep flavors, such as chocolate.

CRUST
2 cups walnuts, soaked and dehydrated
1/4 cup cacao powder
3 tablespoons maple syrup
1 tablespoon coconut oil, melted
1 teaspoon vanilla extract
1/2 teaspoon salt

FILLING
1 cup cashews
1/2 cup raw walnut butter
1/2 cup maple syrup
1/2 teaspoon vanilla extract
1/4 teaspoon salt
1/2 cup coconut oil, melted

SWIRL
1 cup cacao powder
1/2 cup maple syrup
1/2 cup coconut oil, melted

To make the crust, place prepared walnuts in a food processor and pulse into a coarse flour. Add remaining ingredients and lightly pulse until well mixed. Press into a 9-inch tart pan with a removable bottom. Chill until ready to use.

To make the filling, blend all ingredients except coconut oil in a Vita-Mix until smooth. Then add the coconut oil and blend until completely combined, but do not overblend.

To make the swirl, blend all ingredients until smooth.

Pour filling into prepared crust. Allow to chill for 10 minutes until slightly firm. Then pour the swirl on top. Using a chopstick or thin knife, gently swirl the cacao-maple mixture into the filling, making sure not to disrupt the bottom layer of crust. Chill for at least 30 minutes before serving.

MAKES 1 (9-INCH) TART

lemon curd tart

Lemon curd is also excellent on its own or as a topping for fresh berries.

CRUST
2 cups macadamia nuts
½ cup shredded coconut
3 tablespoons agave nectar, maple syrup, or honey
1 teaspoon vanilla extract
½ teaspoon salt

FILLING
2 cups Irish moss paste (see page 18)
1 cup lemon juice
1 cup agave nectar, maple syrup, or honey
½ cup cashews, soaked
1 teaspoon vanilla extract
Pinch turmeric
½ cup coconut oil, melted

To make the crust, place macadamia nuts in a food processor and pulse into a coarse flour. Add remaining ingredients and lightly pulse until well mixed. Press into a 9-inch tart pan with a removable bottom. Refrigerate until ready to use.

To make the filling, blend Irish moss paste, lemon juice, and agave nectar in a Vita-Mix until smooth. Add cashews, vanilla, and turmeric and continue to blend until smooth and creamy. Add coconut oil last and blend until well combined.

Pour filling into prepared crust. Allow to chill for at least an hour before serving.

MAKES 1 (9-INCH) TART

strawberry mascarpone tart

Like many, my first experience with mascarpone cheese was by eating tiramisu, the famous Italian dessert. I later learned how good it was with fruit, particularly berries. Our version avoids the dairy, but retains the neutral yet elegant flavor.

CRUST
1 cup almonds, soaked and dehydrated
1 cup cashews
3 tablespoons agave nectar, maple syrup, or honey
1 teaspoon vanilla extract
1/2 teaspoon salt

MASCARPONE FILLING
2 cups cashews, soaked 1 to 2 hours
1/2 cup water
1/4 cup lemon juice
1/4 cup agave nectar, maple syrup, or honey
1 teaspoon nutritional yeast
1 teaspoon miso
Pinch sea salt

STRAWBERRY LAYER
2 cups sliced strawberries
1/2 cup agave nectar, maple syrup, or honey
2 teaspoons lemon juice
Pinch sea salt

To make the crust, place prepared almonds and cashews in a food processor and pulse into a coarse flour. Add remaining ingredients and lightly pulse until well mixed. Press into a 9-inch tart pan with a removable bottom.

To make the filling, blend all ingredients in a Vita-Mix until smooth.

For the strawberry layer, toss sliced fruit with agave nectar, lemon juice, and salt.

Pour filling into prepared crust and arrange sliced fruit on top.

MAKES 1 (9-INCH) TART

stone fruit pie

The ripeness and choice of the stone fruit used may greatly alter the sweetness of this dish. If using a lot of cherries, for example, it is a good idea to use the agave a bit more sparingly.

CRUST
2¼ cups almonds, soaked
    overnight and dehydrated
3 tablespoons agave nectar, maple syrup, or honey
1 tablespoon coconut oil, melted
¼ teaspoon salt

FILLING
3 cups cashews, soaked 1 to 2 hours
½ cup lemon juice
¾ cup agave nectar, maple syrup, or honey
1 tablespoon vanilla extract

1 teaspoon salt
1 vanilla bean, scraped
1 teaspoon cinnamon
¼ teaspoon nutmeg
¾ cup coconut oil, melted

TOPPING
2 cups sliced mixed stone fruit, such as
    plums, apricots, peaches, or cherries
¼ cup agave nectar, maple syrup, or honey
1 tablespoon lemon juice

To make the crust, place prepared almonds in a food processor and pulse into a coarse flour. Add the remaining ingredients and lightly pulse until well mixed. Press into a 9-inch tart pan with a removable bottom.

To make the filling, blend all ingredients except coconut oil in a Vita-Mix until smooth.

Then add the coconut oil and blend until completely combined, but do not overblend.

To make the fruit topping, toss sliced fruit with agave nectar and lemon juice. Pour filling into crust, then arrange sliced fruit on top.

MAKES 1 (9-INCH) PIE

candied walnut tart

This reminds me of a raw food variation on pecan pie. In fact, pecans work equally well, especially around Thanksgiving.

CRUST
2 cups candied nuts, plus ¹⁄₂ cup
  for garnish (see page 20)
3 tablespoons maple syrup
1 tablespoon coconut oil, melted
1 teaspoon vanilla extract
¹⁄₂ teaspoon salt

FILLING
1 cup cashews
¹⁄₂ cup walnuts, soaked
¹⁄₂ cup maple syrup
¹⁄₄ cup honey
¹⁄₂ teaspoon vanilla extract
1 teaspoon cinnamon
¹⁄₄ teaspoon nutmeg
¹⁄₄ teaspoon salt
¹⁄₂ cup coconut oil, melted

To make the crust, place prepared nuts in a food processor and pulse. Add remaining ingredients and lightly pulse until well mixed. Press into a 9-inch tart pan with a removable bottom. Chill until ready to use.

To make the filling, blend all ingredients except coconut oil in a Vita-Mix until smooth. Then add the coconut oil and blend until completely combined, but do not overblend.

Pour filling into prepared crust. Allow to chill for 10 minutes until slightly firm. Then garnish with remaining candied nuts. Chill for at least 30 minutes before serving.

MAKES 1 (9-INCH) TART

key lime pie

If key limes are not available, lime juice with an extra dose of agave will do the trick.

CRUST
1 cup macadamia nuts
1 cup cashews
1/2 cup shredded coconut
1 teaspoon vanilla extract
1/2 teaspoon salt

FILLING
1 1/2 cups soaked cashews
1/2 cup young coconut meat
1/2 cup key lime juice
3/4 cup agave nectar, maple syrup, or honey
2 tablespoons nut milk
7 tablespoons coconut butter, melted
3 tablespoons vanilla extract
Pinch salt

To make the crust, place macadamia nuts and cashews in a food processor and pulse into a coarse flour. Add remaining ingredients and lightly pulse until well mixed. Press into a 9-inch tart pan with a removable bottom. Refrigerate until ready to use.

To make the filling, blend the first six ingredients until smooth. Then add the coconut butter, vanilla, and salt and blend until completely combined, but do not overblend.

Pour filling into prepared crust and chill before serving.

MAKES 1 (9-INCH) PIE

pear frangipane

Meredith brilliantly balanced this dish, creating the luxurious character of frangipane from almond pulp and Irish moss paste. The filling would also be great inside a raw cookie or brownie.

CRUST

2½ cups cashew flour

2 tablespoons sucanat or maple sugar powder (see page 15)

1 tablespoon agave nectar, maple syrup, or honey

1 tablespoon coconut oil, melted

1 teaspoon vanilla extract

½ teaspoon salt

FILLING

2 cups almond pulp (reserved from almond milk, but not dehydrated)

3 vanilla beans, scraped

¼ cup Irish moss paste (see page 18)

½ cup honey

½ cup agave nectar, maple syrup, or honey

¼ cup agave powder

1 tablespoon vanilla extract

2 teaspoons almond extract

½ teaspoon salt

FRUIT TOPPING

2 pears, sliced

1 cup agave nectar, maple syrup, or honey

2 tablespoons lemon juice

1 teaspoon vanilla extract

1 teaspoon salt

GLAZE

¼ cup agave nectar, maple syrup, or honey or more if needed

To make the crust, lightly pulse all ingredients in the food processor until well combined. Press into a 9-inch tart pan. Chill until ready to use.

To make the filling, in a large mixing bowl mix all ingredients by hand. It should be a moist spongy mixture.

For the fruit topping, toss pears with other ingredients. Place in the dehydrator for 3 to 4 hours or until soft, but not dry. Strain off liquid before using.

Pour or spoon almond filling into prepared crust. Arrange pears on top. Glaze with agave before serving.

MAKES 1 (9-INCH) TART

cakes and cheesecakes

triple layer cacao cake 90

caramel pecan cake 92

german chocolate cake 93

candied carrot-ginger cake 94

spiced pineapple cake with banana cream 95

cupcakes with assorted frosting 96

cinnamon graham cracker fudge cake 98

gingerbread with lemon glaze 99

cacao cake with lavender 100

tres leches 102

maple cheesecake with walnut crust 103

frozen berry cheesecake 104

mango lime cheesecake 106

cinnamon cheesecake 107

triple layer cacao cake

Every raw chef has a favorite chocolate cake recipe. I was very impressed with this version that Meredith designed.

WET INGREDIENTS

3 cups date paste (see page 18)
½ cup almond milk
½ cup agave nectar, maple syrup, or honey
5 tablespoons vanilla extract
½ cup coconut oil, melted

DRY INGREDIENTS

4 cups almond flour
4 cups hazelnut flour
1 cup coconut powder
1 cup cacao powder
1 teaspoon salt

¼ cup Irish moss paste (see page 18) can be used with wet ingredients or ¼ cup flax meal with the dry. This is optional and creates a fluffier mixture.

FUDGE FROSTING

2 cups cashew flour
2 cups almond milk
½ cup maple syrup
4 tablespoons vanilla extract
1 cup cacao powder
¼ teaspoon salt
¾ cup coconut oil, melted
Chocolate maple glaze (see page 15)

WET INGREDIENTS

In a Vita-Mix thoroughly blend all the wet ingredients except for the coconut oil until smooth. Then add the coconut oil and continue to blend until well combined.

CAKE BATTER

In a mixer or food processor mix the dry ingredients until thoroughly combined.

Slowly add the wet ingredients. It is better to use a standing mixer as this will keep the mixture lighter and more fluffy, but if you do not have a standing mixer the batter can be made in a food processor if you lightly pulse the wet ingredients in. You do not want a dense, heavily blended mixture.

FROSTING

In a Vita-Mix thoroughly blend all the ingredients except for the coconut oil and chocolate maple glaze until smooth. Then add the coconut oil and continue to blend until well combined and creamy. Place in the refrigerator for 30 minutes to an hour until slightly firm, but still spreadable.

ASSEMBLY

Divide cake batter into fourths. Press one layer of batter in a 9-inch springform pan and alternate with frosting. Refrigerate until just before serving and glaze with chocolate maple glaze.

MAKES 1 (9-INCH) CAKE

caramel pecan cake

Classic flavor presented in a entirely new way.

WET INGREDIENTS

WET INGREDIENTS

¾ cup pecan milk
3 cups date paste (see page 18)
4 tablespoons vanilla extract
1 teaspoon salt
½ cup coconut oil, melted

DRY INGREDIENTS

4 cups pecan flour
4 cups almond flour
1 cup shredded coconut (powdered in Vita-Mix)
1 cup pecans, chopped

¼ cup Irish moss paste (see page 18) can be used with wet ingredients or ¼ cup flax meal with the dry. This is optional and creates a fluffier mixture.

PECAN CARAMEL FROSTING

1½ cups pecans, soaked
½ cup macadamia nuts
¼ cup pine nuts
1 cup pecan milk
1¼ cups agave nectar, maple syrup, or honey
2 tablespoons lemon juice
1 tablespoon vanilla extract
1 teaspoon cinnamon
¼ teaspoon salt
1 cup coconut oil, melted

WET INGREDIENTS

In a Vita-Mix thoroughly blend all the wet ingredients except for the coconut oil until smooth. Then add the coconut oil and continue to blend until well combined.

CAKE BATTER

In a mixer or food processor mix the dry ingredients until thoroughly combined.

Slowly add the wet ingredients. It is better to use a standing mixer as this will keep the mixture lighter and more fluffy, but if you do not have a standing mixer the batter can be made in a food processor if you lightly pulse the wet ingredients in. You do not want a dense, heavily blended mixture.

FROSTING

In a Vita-Mix thoroughly blend all the ingredients except for the coconut oil until smooth. Then add the coconut oil and continue to blend until well combined and creamy. Place in the refrigerator for 30 minutes to an hour until slightly firm, but still spreadable.

ASSEMBLY

Divide cake batter in half. Press one layer of batter in a 9-inch springform pan and spread with one third of the frosting. Add second cake layer. Refrigerate until just before serving, remove from springform, and frost top and sides with remaining frosting.

MAKES 1 (9-INCH) CAKE

german chocolate cake

I was very happy to reacquaint with my cake of choice for birthdays when I was young.

WET INGREDIENTS
3 cups date paste (see page 18)
½ cup almond milk
½ cup agave nectar, maple syrup, or honey
5 tablespoons vanilla extract
½ cup coconut oil, melted

DRY INGREDIENTS
7 cups almond flour
2 cups shredded coconut (powdered in Vita-Mix)
1 cup cacao powder
1 teaspoon salt

¼ cup Irish moss paste (see page 18) can be used with wet ingredients or ¼ cup flax meal with the dry. This is optional and creates a fluffier mixture.

PECAN COCONUT FROSTING
2 cups cashew flour
1½ cups pecan milk
1 cup agave nectar, maple syrup, or honey
4 tablespoons vanilla extract
Pinch salt
¾ cup coconut oil, melted
1 cup chopped pecans
2 cups shredded coconut
1 cup caramel (see page 21) (optional)

WET INGREDIENTS

In a Vita-Mix thoroughly blend all the wet ingredients except for the coconut oil until smooth. Then add the coconut oil and continue to blend until well combined.

CAKE BATTER

In a mixer or food processor mix the dry ingredients until thoroughly combined. Slowly add the wet ingredients. It is better to use a standing mixer as this will keep the mixture lighter and more fluffy, but if you do not have a standing mixer the batter can be made in a food processor if you lightly pulse the wet ingredients in. You do not want a dense, heavily blended mixture.

FROSTING

In a Vita-Mix thoroughly blend the first five ingredients until smooth. Then add the coconut oil and continue to blend until well combined and creamy. Stir in chopped pecans and shredded coconut. Place in the refrigerator for 30 minutes to an hour until slightly firm, but still spreadable.

ASSEMBLY

Divide cake batter into thirds. Press one layer of batter in a 9-inch springform pan and alternate with frosting until you have made three layers. Refrigerate until just before serving. To make the cake extra decadent, serve with caramel.

MAKES 1 (9-INCH) CAKE

candied carrot-ginger cake

Admittedly, I'm not a raisin fan, but Meredith is, and nearly everyone loves a good carrot cake.

WET INGREDIENTS
3 cups date paste (see page 18)
¼ cup ginger juice
½ cup apple juice
2 tablespoons vanilla extract
½ cup coconut oil, melted

DRY INGREDIENTS
7 cups almond flour
1 cup pecans, soaked and dehydrated
1 cup walnuts, soaked and dehydrated
2½ cups shredded carrots
¾ cup raisins, chopped
1½ tablespoons cinnamon
1 tablespoon grated ginger
1 teaspoon nutmeg
1 teaspoon cloves
1 teaspoon salt

¼ cup Irish moss paste (see page 18) can be used with wet ingredients or ¼ cup flax meal with the dry. This is optional and creates a fluffier mixture.

GINGER CREAM FROSTING
1½ cups cashew flour
½ cup macadamia nuts
1 cup almond milk
1 cup agave nectar, maple syrup, or honey
3 tablespoons ginger juice
1 tablespoon grated ginger
¼ cup lemon juice
1 tablespoon vanilla extract
¼ teaspoon salt
1 cup coconut oil, melted

WET INGREDIENTS
In a Vita-Mix thoroughly blend all the wet ingredients except for the coconut oil until smooth. Then add the coconut oil and continue to blend until well combined.

CAKE BATTER
In a mixer or food processor mix the almond flour, pecans, and walnuts until thoroughly combined. You want the walnuts and pecans to still be slightly chunky. Mix the carrots, raisins, and spices in the mixing bowl of a standing mixer. You do not want to overprocess these ingredients. Slowly add the wet ingredients. Do not make this cake in a food processor. If you do not have a standing mixer this recipe is best mixed by hand so that it remains fluffy and crumbly.

FROSTING
In a Vita-Mix thoroughly blend all the wet ingredients except for the coconut oil until smooth. Then add the coconut oil and continue to blend until well combined and creamy. Place in the refrigerator for 30 minutes to an hour until slightly firm, but still spreadable.

ASSEMBLY
Divide cake batter in half. Press one layer of batter in a 9-inch springform pan and alternate with one third of the frosting. Add second cake layer. Refrigerate until just before serving, remove from springform, and frost with remaining frosting.

MAKES 1 (9-INCH) CAKE

spiced pineapple cake with banana cream

I can't read this recipe without wanting to eat it.

WET INGREDIENTS

2 mashed bananas
½ cup chopped pineapple
3 cups date paste (see page 18)
¼ cup almond milk
2 tablespoons vanilla extract
Pinch salt
½ cup coconut oil, melted

DRY INGREDIENTS

7 cups Brazil nut flour
1 cup shredded coconut (powdered in Vita-Mix)
1 tablespoon cinnamon
½ teaspoon ginger
1 teaspoon nutmeg
Pinch cloves
1 vanilla bean, scraped
1 teaspoon salt

¼ cup Irish moss paste (see page 18) can be used with wet ingredients or ¼ cup flax meal with the dry. This is optional and creates a fluffier mixture.

BANANA CREAM

2 cups cashew flour
1 cup almond milk
2 mashed bananas
¾ cup agave nectar, maple syrup, or honey
¼ cup lemon juice
1 tablespoon vanilla extract
1 cup coconut oil, melted
2 tablespoons coconut butter, melted
Pinch salt

WET INGREDIENTS

In a Vita-Mix thoroughly blend all the wet ingredients except for the coconut oil until smooth. Then add the coconut oil and continue to blend until well combined.

CAKE BATTER

In a mixer or food processor mix the dry ingredients until thoroughly combined. Slowly add the wet ingredients. It is better to use a standing mixer as this will keep the mixture lighter and more fluffy, but if you do not have a standing mixer the batter can be made in a food processor if you lightly pulse the wet ingredients in. You do not want a dense, heavily blended mixture.

FROSTING

In a Vita-Mix thoroughly blend all the wet ingredients except for the coconut oil and coconut butter until smooth. Then add the coconut oil and coconut butter and continue to blend until well combined and creamy. Place in the refrigerator for 30 minutes to an hour until slightly firm, but still spreadable.

ASSEMBLY

Divide cake batter in half. Press one layer of batter in a 9-inch springform pan and alternate with one third of the frosting. Add second cake layer. Refrigerate until just before serving, remove from springform, and frost with remaining frosting.

MAKES 1 (9-INCH) CAKE

cupcakes with assorted frosting

All of our cake recipes can be converted into cupcakes using the same formula for making the cake batter. Instead of using a springform pan, line standard muffin pans with cupcake papers and fill with batter. You can either use the frosting that accompanies the cake or for a more traditional frosting that can be used in a piping bag, use the following recipe.

PIPING FROSTING
2 cups cashew flour
½ cup coconut milk
¼ cup agave nectar, maple syrup, or honey
1 teaspoon vanilla extract
Pinch salt
¼ cup coconut oil, melted
¼ cup coconut butter, melted

FOR FOOD COLORING ADD PER BATCH
Pink: 2 tablespoons beet juice + 1 tablespoon agave nectar, maple syrup, or honey
Green: 2 tablespoons spinach juice+ 1 tablespoon agave nectar, maple syrup, or honey
Yellow: 2 teaspoons turmeric
Chocolate: approximately ¼ cup cacao powder + 2 tablespoons agave nectar, maple syrup, or honey

FROSTING
In a Vita-Mix thoroughly blend all the ingredients except for the coconut oil and coconut butter until smooth. Then add the coconut oil and coconut butter and continue to blend until well combined and creamy. Place in the refrigerator for 30 minutes to an hour until slightly firm. Put in piping bag and frost cupcakes. Keep cupcakes in the refrigerator until ready to serve.

MAKES 3 CUPS FROSTING

cinnamon graham cracker fudge cake

If there were a raw cake variation on s'mores, this would be it.

WET INGREDIENTS

3½ cups date paste (see page 18)
1 cup almond milk
1 tablespoon salt
1 tablespoon vanilla extract
1 cup coconut oil, melted

DRY INGREDIENTS

5 cups almond flour
3 cups cashew flour
1 cup shredded coconut (powdered in Vita-Mix)
1 cup cacao powder
2 tablespoons cinnamon
2 teaspoons salt
¼ cup sucanat or maple sugar powder (see page 15)

GRAHAM CRACKER CRUMBLE

2 cups cashew flour
½ cup sucanat or maple sugar powder (see page 15)
1 teaspoon vanilla extract
2 teaspoons salt

CINNAMON FROSTING

2 cups cashew flour
1½ cups almond milk
1 cup agave nectar, maple syrup, or honey
1 tablespoon lemon juice
2 tablespoons cinnamon
2 teaspoons vanilla extract
2 teaspoons salt
1 cup coconut oil, melted

WET INGREDIENTS

In a Vita-Mix thoroughly blend all the wet ingredients except for the coconut oil until smooth. Then add the coconut oil and continue to blend until well combined.

CAKE BATTER

In a mixer or food processor mix the dry ingredients until thoroughly combined. Slowly add the wet ingredients. It is better to use a standing mixer as this will keep the mixture lighter and more fluffy, but if you do not have a standing mixer the batter can be made in a food processor if you lightly pulse the wet ingredients in. You do not want a dense, heavily blended mixture.

GRAHAM CRACKER CRUMBLE

Mix all ingredients in a food processor until well combined.

FROSTING

In a Vita-Mix thoroughly blend all the ingredients except for the coconut oil until smooth. Then add the coconut oil and continue to blend until well combined and creamy. Place in the refrigerator for 30 minutes to an hour until slightly firm, but still spreadable.

ASSEMBLY

Press half of the batter into a 9-inch springform pan. Sprinkle with crumble. Press remaining batter into pan. Refrigerate for 30 minutes before frosting.

MAKES 1 (9-INCH) CAKE

gingerbread with lemon glaze

Gingerbread is great for holidays—this recipe is also good for breakfast with or without the glaze.

GINGERBREAD

2 cups almond flour
½ cup coconut flour
½ cup flax meal
1 teaspoon cinnamon
½ teaspoon nutmeg
¼ teaspoon cloves
½ teaspoon salt
½ cup date paste (see page 18)
¼ cup agave nectar, maple syrup, or honey
1 tablespoon vanilla extract

1 tablespoon freshly grated ginger
2 tablespoons coconut oil, melted
½ cup nut milk
½ cup raisins, chopped

LEMON GLAZE

1 cup agave nectar, maple syrup, or honey
½ cup macadamia nuts
½ cup lemon juice
1 teaspoon vanilla extract
Pinch salt

GINGERBREAD

In a mixer combine first seven ingredients until well combined. Then add the date paste, agave nectar, vanilla, and ginger and continue to mix. Then slowly add the coconut oil and nut milk. You want the mixture to be fluffy and sticky, but not oily or soupy. Mix in the raisins. By hand, form dough into a loaf-shaped log.

LEMON GLAZE

Blend all ingredients until smooth.

Frost with approximately ½ cup of the lemon glaze and slice into approximately 12 slices. Dehydrate without Teflex for 6 to 8 hours or overnight.

Serve warm out of the dehydrator with a drizzle of lemon juice.

MAKES 12 SERVINGS

cacao cake with lavender

Cacao is intense and occasionally balances nicely with herbal or savory flavors. Lavender is a perfect foil for its richness.

CRUST

2 cups almonds, soaked and dehydrated
¼ cup cacao powder
3 tablespoons agave nectar, maple syrup, or honey
1 tablespoon coconut oil, melted
1 teaspoon vanilla extract
¼ teaspoon salt

FILLING

3 cups cashew flour
1½ cups nut milk
1 cup agave nectar, maple syrup, or honey
3 tablespoons lemon juice
1 vanilla bean, scraped
1 teaspoon vanilla extract
2 tablespoons dried lavender flowers
1 teaspoon cinnamon
Pinch salt
½ cup coconut oil, melted
⅓ cup cacao oil, melted

CRUST

Process the cashews in a food processor to a fine meal. Add cacao powder and remaining ingredients until combined. Do not overprocess; you want the mixture to be crumbly. Press crust into a 9-inch springform pan.

FILLING

Blend all ingredients except oils until smooth. Then add oils and continue to blend until well combined.

ASSEMBLY

Pour filling into crust and refrigerate for at least an hour before serving.

MAKES 1 (9-INCH) CAKE

tres leches

Tres Leches translates as "three milks" from Spanish and could be described as a cake-pudding. It is intentionally wet, which makes it not only refreshing but surprisingly light.

WET INGREDIENTS
3 cups date paste (see page 18)
1 cup almond milk
3 tablespoons vanilla extract
¼ teaspoon salt
⅔ cup coconut oil, melted

DRY INGREDIENTS
5 cups almond flour
3 cups shredded coconut (powdered in Vita-Mix)
2 tablespoons cinnamon
3 vanilla beans, scraped

¼ cup Irish moss paste (see page 18) can be used with wet ingredients or ¼ cup flax meal with the dry. This is optional and creates a fluffier mixture.

VANILLA CUSTARD
2 cups cashews, soaked
1 cup young coconut meat
1 cup agave nectar, maple syrup, or honey
¼ cup Irish moss paste (see page 18)
2 tablespoons lemon juice
1 tablespoon vanilla extract
1 vanilla bean, scraped
1 teaspoon cinnamon
½ teaspoon salt
Water, added 1 tablespoon at a
    time if needed to blend
1 cup coconut butter, melted

VANILLA CRÈME FROSTING
2 cups cashew flour
1 cup almond milk
1 cup young coconut meat
1 cup agave nectar, maple syrup, or honey
1 tablespoon lemon juice
1 teaspoon vanilla extract
Pinch salt
1 cup coconut oil, melted

WET INGREDIENTS
In a Vita-Mix thoroughly blend all the wet ingredients except for the coconut oil until smooth. Then add the coconut oil and continue to blend until well combined.

CAKE BATTER
In a mixer or food processor mix the dry ingredients until thoroughly combined. Slowly add the wet ingredients. It is better to use a standing mixer as this will keep the mixture lighter and more fluffy, but if you do not have a standing mixer the batter can be made in a food processor if you lightly pulse the wet ingredients in. You do not want a dense, heavily blended mixture.

VANILLA CUSTARD
In a Vita-Mix thoroughly blend all the wet ingredients except for the coconut butter until smooth. Then add the coconut butter and continue to blend until well combined and creamy.

VANILLA CRÈME FROSTING
Follow same directions as custard.

ASSEMBLY
Divide cake batter in half. Press one layer of batter in a 9-inch springform pan. Pour in custard. Add second cake layer. Refrigerate until just before serving, remove from springform, and frost with vanilla crème frosting.

MAKES 1 (9-INCH) CAKE

maple cheesecake with walnut crust

Many of our raw recipes are inspired by classic flavors from other dishes—in this case, maple walnut ice cream.

CRUST

2 cups walnuts, soaked and dehydrated
2 tablespoons agave nectar, maple syrup, or honey
2 tablespoons sucanat or maple sugar powder (see page 15)
1 teaspoon vanilla extract
½ teaspoon salt

FILLING

3 cups cashew flour
2 cups nut milk
1 cup maple syrup
3 tablespoons lemon juice
2 tablespoons vanilla extract
¼ teaspoon salt
1 cup coconut oil, melted

CRUST

Process the walnuts in a food processor to a fine meal. Add remaining ingredients until combined. Do not overprocess; you want the mixture to be crumbly. Press crust into a 9-inch springform pan.

FILLING

Blend all ingredients except for oil until smooth. Then add oil and continue to blend until well combined.

ASSEMBLY

Pour filling into crust and chill for an hour before serving.

MAKES 1 (9-INCH) CHEESECAKE

frozen berry cheesecake

This is an all-purpose cheesecake that is great with any seasonal berries or a combination of berries.

CRUST
2 cups cashews
3 tablespoons agave nectar, maple syrup, or honey
½ teaspoon vanilla extract
1 teaspoon salt

FILLING
3 cups cashew flour
2 cups nut milk
½ cup lemon juice
¼ cup lime juice

1 cup agave nectar, maple syrup, or honey
1 tablespoon vanilla extract
Pinch salt
½ cup coconut oil, melted

BERRY SWIRL
1 cup fresh or frozen berries
1 teaspoon lemon juice
½ cup agave nectar, maple syrup, or honey
¼ cup coconut oil, melted

CRUST
Process the cashews in a food processor to a fine meal. Add remaining ingredients until combined. Do not overprocess; you want the mixture to be crumbly. Press crust into a 9-inch springform pan.

FILLING
Blend all ingredients except for coconut oil until smooth. Then add oil and continue to blend until well combined.

SWIRL
Blend all ingredients except for coconut oil until smooth. Then add oil and continue to blend until well combined.

ASSEMBLY
Pour filling into crust and refrigerate for about 20 minutes until slightly firm. Pour berry swirl on top and swirl in using a chopstick or another thin utensil being careful not to disturb the crust. Chill for an hour before serving.

MAKES 1 (9-INCH) CHEESECAKE

mango lime cheesecake

Mango, papaya, oranges, and other creamy, sweet fruits balance well with the tartness of citrus. Mandarin oranges also work well in this recipe.

CRUST
1½ cups macadamia nuts
1 cup shredded coconut
3 tablespoons agave nectar, maple syrup, or honey
1 teaspoon vanilla extract
1 teaspoon salt

FILLING
3 cups cashews, soaked
4 cups chopped fresh mango
1 cup nut milk
½ cup agave nectar, maple syrup, or honey
⅓ cup lime juice
1 tablespoon vanilla extract
Pinch salt
Pinch cinnamon
Pinch cayenne
1 cup coconut oil, melted

CRUST
Process the macadamia nuts and shredded coconut in a food processor to a fine meal. Add remaining ingredients until combined. Do not overprocess; you want the mixture to be crumbly. Press crust into a 9-inch springform pan.

FILLING
Blend all ingredients except for coconut oil until smooth. Then add oil and continue to blend until well combined.

ASSEMBLY
Pour filling into crust and chill for an hour before serving.

MAKES 1 (9-INCH) CHEESECAKE

cinnamon cheesecake

The swirling technique below is fast, simple, and adds tremendously to the presentation.

CRUST
2 cups almond flour
3 tablespoons agave nectar, maple syrup, or honey
1 teaspoon vanilla extract
1 teaspoon salt

FILLING
3½ cups cashew flour
¾ cup agave nectar, maple syrup, or honey
¾ cup almond milk
3 tablespoons lemon juice

2 vanilla beans, scraped
1 teaspoon cinnamon
½ teaspoon nutmeg
½ teaspoon salt
1 cup coconut oil, melted

CINNAMON SWIRL
½ cup maple syrup
1 teaspoon vanilla extract
1 teaspoon cinnamon
¼ teaspoon salt

CRUST
Process the almonds in a food processor to a fine meal. Add remaining ingredients until combined. Do not overprocess; you want the mixture to be crumbly. Press crust into a 9-inch springform pan.

FILLING
Blend all ingredients except coconut oil until smooth. Then add oil and continue to blend until well combined.

SWIRL
Blend all ingredients until smooth.

ASSEMBLY
Pour filling into crust and refrigerate for about 20 minutes until slightly firm. Pour maple mixture on top and swirl in using a chopstick or another thin utensil, being careful not to disturb the crust. Chill for an hour before serving.

MAKES 1 (9-INCH) CHEESECAKE

comfort

apple cider donut holes

If you like, you can make the entire donut instead of just the holes using the same process described here and a donut mold. But these are more fun in smaller bites.

4 cups almond flour
1 cup coconut powder + ¼ cup for dusting
½ teaspoon salt
1 teaspoon cinnamon + 1 tablespoon for dusting
½ teaspoon nutmeg
¼ teaspoon ground cloves

1 cup chopped apples
½ cup date paste (see page 18)
½ cup coconut oil, melted
½ cup apple juice
1 teaspoon vanilla extract

In a mixer combine flour, coconut powder, salt, and spices until well mixed. Then add the apples, date paste, coconut oil, apple juice, and vanilla and continue to mix. You want the mixture to be fluffy and sticky, but not oily or soupy. Once a doughlike consistency is achieved, roll mixture into 2-inch round balls using your hands.

Dehydrate for 6 to 8 hours or overnight. You want the donut holes to be slightly firm on the outside, but still soft and chewy on the inside. Dust with reserved coconut powder and cinnamon.

MAKES ABOUT 2 DOZEN DONUT HOLES

banana-cacao pancakes

Try these wrapped around sweetened raw almond butter as a great dessert for children.

2 ripe bananas
2 cups pecans, soaked
2 cups cashews, soaked
1 cup water
½ cup agave nectar, maple syrup, or honey
1 vanilla bean, scraped

1 teaspoon cinnamon
1 teaspoon salt
2 tablespoons Irish moss paste (see page 18)
1½ cups maple syrup
1 tablespoon flax meal
½ cup cacao nibs

Blend all ingredients except flax meal and cacao nibs in a Vita-Mix until smooth. Stir in flax meal and cacao nibs. Spread batter into 5-inch rounds on Teflex sheets. Pancakes should be thin.

Dehydrate at least 24 hours. Serve with warm maple syrup and sliced bananas.

MAKES 10 SERVINGS

banana-coconut fruit crepes

Some raw desserts would be equally delicious for breakfast; this is a great pancake alternative.

CREPES
1/2 cup mashed banana
1/4 cup chopped young coconut meat
1/2 cup shredded coconut
1 tablespoon lemon juice
1 cup water
1 tablespoon coconut oil, melted
1/4 cup agave nectar, maple syrup, or honey
1 teaspoon vanilla extract
1/2 teaspoon salt
1/2 cup flax meal

FILLING
4 cups sliced mixed fruit (bananas, strawberries, blueberries, and so on)
1/4 cup agave nectar, maple syrup, or honey + more for serving
1 teaspoon lemon juice
1 vanilla bean, scraped
Pinch salt

To make the crepes, blend all ingredients except flax meal until smooth. Add the flax meal and continue to blend until well incorporated. Spread into 6- to 7-inch rounds on dehydrator sheets. Dehydrate 5 to 6 hours, until dry but pliable.

To make the filling, toss fruit with agave nectar, lemon juice, vanilla, and salt.

Fill each crepe with approximately 1/2 cup of filling. Drizzle with agave.

MAKES 8 SERVINGS

vanilla angel food cake

Angel food cake is good served plain or with a simple syrup, such as agave with a touch of citrus juice.

WET INGREDIENTS
3 cups date paste (see page 18)
¾ cup nut milk
1 vanilla bean, scraped
1 teaspoon vanilla extract
½ teaspoon salt
½ cup coconut oil, melted

DRY INGREDIENTS
7 cups shredded coconut
4 cups almond flour

¼ cup Irish moss paste (see page 18) can be used with wet ingredients or ¼ cup flax meal with the dry. This is optional and creates a fluffier mixture.

In a Vita-Mix thoroughly blend all the wet ingredients except coconut oil until smooth. Then add coconut oil and continue to blend until well combined.

In a dry Vita-Mix make a flour out of the shredded coconut. Process to make it as fine as possible. In a food processor or stand mixer, mix the dry ingredients until thoroughly combined. Slowly add the wet ingredients. It is better to use a stand mixer as this will keep the batter lighter and more fluffy, but if you do not have a stand mixer you can make the recipe in a food processor if you just lightly pulse in the wet ingredients. You do not want a dense, heavily blended batter.

Press batter into a 9-inch springform pan. Refrigerate. Just before serving, remove cake from pan. Serve plain, with a simple agave nectar, or with your favorite berries.

MAKES 1 (9-INCH) CAKE

pumpkin pie with shortbread crust

This keeps especially well in the freezer, making it an ideal holiday dessert that can be prepared in advance.

CRUST
1/2 cup shredded coconut
2 cups cashew flour
2 tablespoons agave nectar, maple syrup, or honey
2 tablespoons powdered sucanat or maple sugar
1 teaspoon vanilla extract
1 teaspoon salt

FILLING
1/2 cup cashew flour
3/4 cup agave nectar, maple syrup, or honey
1/2 cup carrot juice
1 tablespoon lemon juice
1 teaspoon vanilla extract
1 vanilla bean, scraped
1 1/2 teaspoons cinnamon
1 teaspoon nutmeg
1/2 teaspoon ginger
Pinch ground cloves
1/4 teaspoon salt
1/2 cup coconut oil, melted

To make the crust, in a dry Vita-Mix make a flour out of the shredded coconut. Process to make it as fine as possible. In a food processor combine coconut flour you've just made, cashew flour, and remaining ingredients for crust. Do not overblend; you want the mixture to be light but to hold together when pressed between your fingers. Press into a 9-inch tart pan and chill until ready to use.

To make the filling, blend all ingredients except coconut oil in a Vita-Mix until smooth. Slowly add coconut oil and continue to blend until well combined.

To assemble, pour filling into prepared crust and refrigerate at least an hour before serving.

MAKES 1 (9-INCH) PIE

blueberry turnovers

The pastry in this recipe includes apple and is nut-free, leaving it light and pliable. Raspberries, blackberries, or cherries are good alternatives in place of the blueberries if you desire.

PASTRY
3 cups shredded apples
$\frac{1}{2}$ cup agave nectar, maple syrup, or honey
$\frac{1}{2}$ cup water
2 tablespoons olive oil
$\frac{1}{2}$ teaspoon cinnamon
1 teaspoon salt
$\frac{3}{4}$ cup flax meal

FILLING
3 cups fresh blueberries, divided
$\frac{1}{2}$ cup agave nectar, maple syrup, or honey
3 tablespoons lemon juice
Pinch salt

To make the pastry, blend all ingredients except flax meal in a Vita-Mix until smooth. Add the flax meal and continue to blend until well incorporated. Spread into 6- to 7-inch rounds on dehydrator sheets. Dehydrate 5 to 6 hours, until dry but pliable.

To make the filling, blend 2 cups blueberries with remaining ingredients in a Vita-Mix until smooth. Stir in reserved 1 cup of blueberries. Place in dehydrator for 2 to 3 hours until mixture begins to thicken.

To assemble the turnovers, fold pastry into quarters creating two pockets for filling. Fill with blueberry filling.

MAKES 6 TO 8 SERVINGS

cherry crisp

Some of the best desserts can often be a bit messy, including crisps. This cherry crisp works nicely when prepared and served in individual cups or ramekins.

CRISP
1 cup walnuts, soaked and dehydrated
1 cup almonds, soaked and dehydrated
1 cup pecans, soaked and dehydrated
¼ cup powdered sucanat or maple sugar
1 teaspoon cinnamon
½ teaspoon nutmeg
¼ teaspoon ginger
1 teaspoon sea salt
1 teaspoon vanilla extract
¼ cup date paste (see page 18)
1 tablespoon coconut oil, melted

BLACK CHERRY FILLING
6 cups fresh or frozen black cherries, divided
¼ cup agave nectar, maple syrup, or honey
1 tablespoon vanilla extract
1 tablespoon lemon juice
1 teaspoon cinnamon
Pinch salt

To make the crisp, pulse nuts, sucanat, spices, and salt in a food processor until well combined but still chunky. Then add vanilla, date paste, and coconut oil; process until crumbly.

To make the filling, blend 3 cups of the cherries with the remaining ingredients in a Vita-Mix until smooth. Then stir in the reserved 3 cups of cherries.

To assemble, sprinkle about one third of the crumble in the bottom of a 9-inch pan or divide among individual cups or ramekins. Lightly press down to form a crust. Then pour the filling over the top. Top loosely with remaining crumble. Dehydrate for 2 to 3 hours. Serve warm.

MAKES 8 TO 10 SERVINGS

pear crisp

Great with cinnamon ice cream!

CRISP

2 cups pecans, soaked and dehydrated
1 cup almonds, soaked and dehydrated
2 tablespoons powdered sucanat or maple sugar
1 teaspoon cinnamon
$\frac{1}{2}$ teaspoon nutmeg
$\frac{1}{8}$ teaspoon ground cloves
1 teaspoon sea salt
1 teaspoon vanilla extract
$\frac{1}{4}$ cup date paste (see page 18)
1 tablespoon coconut oil, melted

PEAR FILLING

6 cups peeled and chopped pears, divided
$\frac{1}{4}$ cup agave nectar, maple syrup, or honey
1 tablespoon vanilla extract
1 tablespoon lemon juice
1 teaspoon cinnamon
$\frac{1}{4}$ teaspoon nutmeg
Pinch ground cloves
Pinch salt

To make crisp, pulse nuts, sucanat, spices, and salt in a food processor until well combined but still chunky. Then add vanilla, date paste, and coconut oil and process until crumbly.

To make filling, blend 3 cups of the pears with remaining ingredients in a food processor until smooth. Then stir in the reserved 3 cups pears.

To assemble, sprinkle about one third of the crumble in the bottom of a 9-inch pan and lightly press down to form a crust. Then pour in the filling. Top loosely with remaining crumble. Dehydrate for 2 to 3 hours. Serve warm with cinnamon ice cream if desired.

MAKES 8 TO 10 SERVINGS

peach crisp

Yellow peaches or even nectarines or plums make good variations for the white peaches in this recipe.

CRISP
2 cups cashews
1 cup almonds, soaked and dehydrated
2 tablespoons sucanat or maple
 sugar powder (see page 15)
1 teaspoon cinnamon
1 teaspoon sea salt
1 teaspoon vanilla extract
¼ cup date paste (see page 18)
1 tablespoon coconut oil, melted

WHITE PEACH FILLING
6 cups sliced fresh white peaches, divided
¼ cup agave nectar, maple syrup, or honey
1 tablespoon vanilla extract
1 tablespoon lemon juice
1 teaspoon cinnamon
Pinch salt

To make crisp, pulse nuts, sucanat, cinnamon, and salt in a food processor or Vita-Mix until well combined but still chunky. Then add vanilla, date paste, and coconut oil and process until crumbly.

To make filling, blend 3 cups of the white peaches with remaining ingredients in a food processor until smooth. Then mix in the remaining 3 cups of sliced peaches.

To assemble, sprinkle about one third of the crumble in the bottom of a 9-inch pan and lightly press down to form a crust. Then pour in the filling. Top loosely with remaining crumble. Dehydrate for 2 to 3 hours. Serve warm.

MAKES 8 TO 10 SERVINGS

apple cobbler with almond crumble

Many comfort desserts benefit from being served warm—this cobbler is delicious that way.

CRUMBLE
2 cups almonds, soaked and dehydrated
2 cups walnuts, soaked and dehydrated
6 tablespoons powdered sucanat or maple sugar
2 teaspoons cinnamon
1 teaspoon nutmeg
1/4 teaspoon ground cloves
1 teaspoon sea salt
1 teaspoon vanilla extract
1/4 cup date paste (see page 18)
1 tablespoon coconut oil, melted

APPLE FILLING
4 to 5 medium-sized apples
1/2 cup agave nectar, maple syrup, or honey
1 teaspoon lemon juice
1 teaspoon vanilla extract
2 teaspoons cinnamon
1 teaspoon nutmeg
Pinch salt

To make the crumble, pulse nuts, sucanat, spices, and salt in a food processor until well combined but still chunky. Then add vanilla, date paste, and coconut oil and process until crumbly.

To make the filling, peel apples and slice as thinly as possible, preferably with a mandoline. Toss apples with remaining ingredients. Dehydrate for approximately 1 hour or until apples are semisoft.

To assemble, line a terrine pan with plastic wrap or parchment. Press one third of the crumble on the bottom to form a crust. Spread in the apple filling and top with remaining crumble. Serve with caramel (see page 21) or vanilla ice cream (see page 138) if desired.

MAKES 8 TO 10 SERVINGS

ice cream and frozen treats

neapolitan ice cream

This is delicate to put together, but easy to serve and the combination of flavors is worth it.

½ cup young coconut meat
1½ cups cashews
½ cup agave nectar, maple syrup, or honey
1 cup almond milk
1 vanilla bean, scraped

½ cup coconut butter, melted
Pinch sea salt
¼ cup pureed strawberries
¼ cup cacao powder

Blend the first seven ingredients in a Vita-Mix until smooth, making a vanilla ice cream base. Divide this mixture into thirds. Stir strawberries into the first portion. Stir cacao powder into the second portion. Leave the third portion as vanilla.

Line a terrine pan with plastic wrap, making sure to leave excess wrap coming over the edges—you will need this in order to remove the ice cream. Pour in the strawberry mixture and freeze. Next pour in the vanilla layer and freeze.

Finally pour in the chocolate mixture and freeze. You want to make sure that each layer is firm before you add the others.

Once the entire terrine is solid you can remove the ice cream from the mold by pulling up on the plastic wrap. Slice ice cream to serve.

MAKES 1 QUART

chocolate cones

Who doesn't think ice cream is better in a cone?

½ cup cacao powder
½ cup young coconut meat
2 teaspoons lemon juice

¾ cup peeled and chopped apple
1½ cups water
1¼ cups flax meal

Blend all ingredients except flax meal in Vita-Mix until smooth. Add flax meal last, as it will start to thicken the mixture. Spread batter thinly into 5- to 6-inch rounds on dehydrator Teflex sheets. Dehydrate 5 to 6 hours until dry but very pliable.

Remove rounds from Teflex sheets and shape each round into a cone. Press edges together. If needed, use paper clips to secure the edges. Place cones on dehydrator screens sheets and dehydrate for 24 more hours until crisp.

MAKES 12 CONES

sesame ice cream

This is like halvah, very rich from the oils in the sesame. You could also substitute black sesame seeds for a bit more contrast.

1 cup cashews
½ cup young coconut meat
½ cup agave nectar, maple syrup, or honey
1¼ cups almond milk or other nut milk
2 tablespoons tahini

1 vanilla bean, scraped
2 tablespoons vanilla extract
¼ cup coconut oil, melted
Pinch salt
3 tablespoons sesame seeds

MAKES 1 QUART

Blend all ingredients except sesame seeds in a Vita-Mix until smooth. Stir in sesame seeds. Pour into an ice cream maker and follow manufacturer's instructions.

hazelnut gelato

The base here could be adjusted to work with almonds, cashews, or pine nuts as well. The absence of coconut meat makes this slightly lighter than our ice cream recipes.

½ cup young coconut meat
1¼ cups hazelnut milk
¾ cup cashews
½ cup agave nectar, maple syrup, or honey

2 tablespoons vanilla extract
1 teaspoon hazelnut extract
½ cup coconut butter, melted
Pinch salt

MAKES 1 QUART

Blend all ingredients in a Vita-Mix until smooth. Pour into an ice cream maker and follow manufacturer's instructions.

banana-toffee ice cream

When aiming to achieve a pleasing texture with raw ice cream, it is always best to first run the ice cream through the ice cream maker and then fold in the firm ingredients after.

TOFFEE
1/2 cup coconut oil, melted
1 cup sucanat or maple sugar powder (see page 15)
1/4 cup agave nectar, maple syrup, or honey
1/2 cup chopped almonds

ICE CREAM
1 cup cashews
1/2 cup young coconut meat
1/2 cup agave nectar, maple syrup, or honey
1 cup almond milk
3/4 cup mashed banana
1 vanilla bean, scraped
1/2 cup coconut butter, melted
Pinch sea salt

To make the toffee, mix all ingredients in a bowl; it should be a sticky thick mixture. Smooth onto a baking sheet and score into small pieces. Place in freezer until firm. Break into small pieces when ready to use.

To make the ice cream, blend all ingredients in a Vita-Mix until smooth. Pour into an ice cream maker and follow manufacturer's instructions. Before the ice cream is fully frozen add the toffee pieces.

MAKES 1 QUART

malted coconut ice cream

Maca, the Peruvian root, has a nutty, malt-like flavor that enhances custards, ice creams, and even chocolate desserts.

1 1/2 cups coconut milk
1/2 cup cashews, soaked
1/2 cup agave nectar, maple syrup, or honey
1/2 cup shredded coconut

4 tablespoons Maca
2 tablespoons vanilla extract
1/4 cup coconut butter, melted
Pinch sea salt

MAKES 1 QUART

Blend all ingredients in a Vita-Mix until smooth. Pour into an ice cream maker and follow manufacturer's instructions.

peach melba

There are many ways to serve Peach Melba—in a glass, a bowl, or even a martini glass. As the colors blend together, it creates a nice sunset, so clear glass is preferred.

VANILLA CRÈME
1 cup cashews
1/2 cup young coconut meat
1/2 cup agave nectar, maple syrup, or honey
1 1/2 cups water
1 tablespoon vanilla extract
1 vanilla bean, scraped
1/2 cup coconut butter, melted
Pinch salt

RASPBERRY SAUCE
1 cup raspberries
1/3 cup agave nectar, maple syrup, or honey
2 tablespoons lemon juice

FOR SERVING
2 cups sliced or pureed peaches

Blend all ingredients for vanilla crème in a Vita-Mix until smooth. You can either freeze in an ice cream maker to make vanilla ice cream or simply place mixture in the freezer. When serving, you want the ice cream to be somewhat melted.

Blend raspberries with agave nectar and lemon juice separately in a Vita-Mix to make a raspberry sauce.

Layer ingredients to make a parfait when serving—first the vanilla crème, then the raspberry sauce, then the sliced or pureed peaches.

MAKES 6 TO 8 SERVINGS

chocolate–chocolate chip ice cream sandwich

These can be made far ahead and stored on wax or parchment paper in the freezer. The recipe also works well and looks great with a green mint or basil ice cream.

4 cups cashew flour
4 cups cacao powder
1 cup agave nectar, maple syrup, or honey
1/2 cup date paste (see page 18)
1/2 cup coconut oil, melted

1 tablespoon vanilla extract
1/2 teaspoon salt
2 quarts chocolate sorbet, softened (see page 136)
Cacao nibs

In a large bowl, mix together cashew flour and cacao powder. Add the next five ingredients and mix well by hand. The mixture should be a dough-like consistency. Using a rolling pin, roll dough in between two sheets of parchment paper into a thin, even layer. Remove top sheet of parchment paper and form cookies either by using a ring mold or cookie cutter. Place in freezer for at least an hour until ready to assemble.

To assemble ice cream sandwiches, scoop approximately 1/2 cup chocolate sorbet in between two cookies and gently press together. Roll the sides of the ice cream sandwich in cacao nibs to coat. Refreeze for at least an hour before serving.

MAKES ABOUT 8 LARGE SANDWICHES

fudgesicle

This concept works with most ice cream bases, so feel free to experiment.

1 cup cashews
1/2 cup young coconut meat
1/2 cup agave nectar, maple syrup, or honey
1 cup almond milk or other nut milk
1/2 cup cacao powder
2 tablespoons vanilla extract
1/2 cup coconut oil, melted
Pinch salt

CHOCOLATE SHELL (OPTIONAL)
1 cup coconut oil
1/2 cup cacao powder
1/2 cup agave nectar, maple syrup, or honey
1 teaspoon salt
1 teaspoon vanilla extract

Blend all ingredients until smooth in a Vita-Mix and pour into Popsicle molds. Freeze overnight. Run hot water over Popsicle molds to help remove easily.

To make the chocolate shell, blend all ingredients in a Vita-Mix until smooth.

If you would like to dip the Popsicles in chocolate, once you remove them from the molds, refreeze, and then dip into melted chocolate. The cold fudgesicles will cause the chocolate to harden immediately.

MAKES 10 TO 12

chocolate sorbet

The addition of almond milk lightens this a bit, creating more of a sorbet-like texture.

1 cup cashews
½ cup young coconut meat
½ cup agave nectar, maple syrup, or honey
1¼ cups almond milk or other nut milk

½ cup cacao powder
2 tablespoons vanilla extract
¼ cup coconut oil, melted
Pinch salt

Blend all ingredients in a Vita-Mix until smooth. Pour into an ice cream maker and follow manufacturer's instructions.

MAKES 1 QUART

pink grapefruit sorbet

This is an ideal refresher after any salty or rich meal.

3 large pink or red grapefruit, chopped,
   with seeds and membranes removed
1 cup agave nectar, maple syrup, or honey
1 frozen banana

3 cups water
1 tablespoon fresh lime juice
1 tablespoon beet juice (optional)

Blend all ingredients in a Vita-Mix until smooth. Pour into an ice cream maker and follow manufacturer's instructions.

MAKES 1 QUART

black cherry sorbet

Our sorbet base also works well with other stone fruits, such as plums, nectarines, peaches, and apricots.

3 cups fresh or frozen pitted black cherries
1 cup agave nectar, maple syrup, or honey
1 frozen banana

3 cups water
1 tablespoon fresh lemon juice
1 tablespoon beet juice (optional)

Blend all ingredients except for 1/2 cup black cherries in a Vita-Mix until smooth. Pour into an ice cream maker and follow manufacturer's instructions. Stir in the reserved 1/2 cup black cherries just before the sorbet is fully frozen.

MAKES 1 QUART

ginger orange julius

Orange Julius was a popular chain when I was growing up. The recipe included a mixture of orange juice, powdered milk, and egg whites. This is a fun variation Meredith created.

1 cup cashews
1/2 cup young coconut meat
1/4 cup agave nectar, maple syrup, or honey
1 cup almond milk
1/2 cup orange juice

1 tablespoon vanilla extract
2 vanilla beans, scraped
1/2 cup coconut butter, melted
2 teaspoons freshly grated ginger
Pinch salt

Blend all ingredients in a Vita-Mix until smooth.

MAKES 4 TO 6 SERVINGS

kombucha float

This is our version of the ice cream float, which is traditionally made with root beer and vanilla ice cream. Kombucha is a fermented tea beverage that is readily available in most health food stores. It comes in various flavors so feel free to experiment with different variations. We preferred to keep it simple on this one—strawberry kombucha and vanilla ice cream.

2 scoops vanilla ice cream
1 bottle of your favorite kombucha

Scoop vanilla ice cream in a tall glass, and carefully fill with kombucha.

You can always experiment with different flavor combinations. Although you can't go wrong with strawberry and vanilla.

MAKES 1 SERVING

vanilla ice cream

Always versatile, always delicious.

½ **cup young coconut meat**
1½ **cups cashews**
½ **cup agave nectar, maple syrup, or honey**
1 cup almond milk

1 vanilla bean, scraped
½ **cup coconut butter, melted**
Pinch sea salt

Blend all ingredients in a Vita-Mix until smooth. Pour into an ice cream maker and follow manufacturer's instructions.

MAKES 1 QUART

index

Metric Conversion Chart

Volume Measurements		Weight Measurements		Temperature Conversion	
U.S.	**METRIC**	**U.S.**	**METRIC**	**FAHRENHEIT**	**CELSIUS**
1 teaspoon	5 ml	1/2 ounce	15 g	250	120
1 tablespoon	15 ml	1 ounce	30 g	300	150
1/4 cup	60 ml	3 ounces	90 g	325	160
1/3 cup	75 ml	4 ounces	115 g	350	180
1/2 cup	125 ml	8 ounces	225 g	375	190
2/3 cup	150 ml	12 ounces	350 g	400	200
3/4 cup	175 ml	1 pound	450 g	425	220
1 cup	250 ml	2 1/4 pounds	1 kg	450	230